THE MAN WHO WAS HANGED BY A THREAD

and Other Tales from BC's First Lawmen

CECIL CLARK

VICTORIA · VANCOUVER · CALGARY

Heritage House Publishing Company Ltd.
www.heritagehouse.ca

Library and Archives Canada Cataloguing in Publication
Clark, Cecil, 1899–
The man who was hanged by a thread: and other tales from BC's first lawmen / Cecil Clark.

(Amazing stories)
Originally published in B.C. Provincial Police stories.
Issued also in electronic format.
ISBN 978-1-926936-94-9

1. B.C. Provincial Police—Biography. 2. B.C. Provincial Police—History. 3. Law enforcement—British Columbia—History. I. Title. II. Series: Amazing stories (Victoria, B.C.)

HV8159.B7C53 2011   363.209711   C2011-905043-9

Series editor: Lesley Reynolds
Cover design: Chyla Cardinal. Interior design: Frances Hunter
Cover photos: Mug shots of Owen Baker (top) and Harry Sowash courtesy of *The Shoulder Strap*

The interior of this book was produced on 100% post-consumer recycled paper, processed chlorine free and printed with vegetable-based inks.

Heritage House acknowledges the financial support for its publishing program from the Government of Canada through the Canada Book Fund (CBF), Canada Council for the Arts and the province of British Columbia through the British Columbia Arts Council and the Book Publishing Tax Credit.

 Canadian Patrimoine
Heritage canadien

 Canada Council Conseil des Arts
for the Arts du Canada

 BRITISH COLUMBIA
ARTS COUNCIL

Printed in Canada

15 14 13 12 11 1 2 3 4 5

To the British Columbia Provincial Police,
the men who served the province so well

Contents

Prologue

IT WAS MAY 6, 1865, *and near the community of Bella Coola on the British Columbia coast, the 80-ton trading schooner* Langley *swung at anchor in a little bay. Forward in the ship's fo'c'sle, an oil lamp swinging in a gimbal cast eerie shadows as skipper Smith poked some wood in the stove preparatory to making coffee. On a locker nearby sat big, bearded BC Provincial Police constable J.D.B. "Jack" Ogilvie, sole representative of the law between Cape Caution and the Skeena River, 200 miles (320 kilometres) as the crow flies, but several thousand along the fjords that characterize the region.*

Ogilvie and his friend Morris Moss, a coastal fur trader, had boarded Langley *in search of a fugitive. A few days earlier, Ogilvie had asked Moss to help him capture some renegades who were selling liquor to the Native people. Among them was a 35-year-old French Canadian named Antoine Lucanage, who on April 1, 1865, boldly sailed right into Bella Coola in broad daylight. He and his boat were seized by Ogilvie, and Lucanage was shipped to jail at New Westminster on a passing schooner.*

On the way, he jumped overboard at the south end of Johnstone Strait and miraculously reached shore despite swirling tide rips. He was later picked up by Langley, *whose skipper was unaware that Lucanage was on his way to jail. By a strange quirk of fate, Bella Coola was among her stopping places. There, Lucanage slipped ashore at night. When Ogilvie heard of the incident he mustered some Natives and searched the area, but they found no trace of the fugitive. When* Langley *left a couple of days later, Ogilvie had a hunch that Lucanage had somehow regained the vessel. "Let's catch her up and search her," was his quick suggestion to Moss. The pair set off and caught up with the schooner about four hours later. Skipper Smith swore that the fugitive wasn't aboard.*

As the men talked, they didn't notice the door of the forward chain locker slowly open. From it peered an evil-looking face, unshaven with eyes deep set and treacherous. The man raised a heavy Colt revolver, levelled it at the unsuspecting police officer and pulled the trigger. The crashing report rocked the little cabin. In an acrid, billowing cloud of black-powder smoke, Ogilvie got slowly to his feet, then slumped down.

Introduction

WHILE IT IS TRUE THAT British Columbia, born of the quest for furs and gold, had the usual early-day frontier society, it was a frontier scene with a difference. It had law and order. Murders were committed, of course, but the culprits were usually apprehended. Then they were swiftly tried and, if found guilty, usually hanged. The first judge on the British Columbia mainland (then called the Colony of British Columbia) was Matthew Baillie Begbie, who later became Chief Justice of British Columbia. He was selected because Sir Edward Bulwer-Lytton, Colonial Secretary in London, wanted a young, athletic man who, in Lytton's own words, "must be a man who could, if necessary, truss a murderer up and hang him from the nearest tree."

While Begbie didn't hang anybody himself, he became the terror of evildoers and a legend who established a formidable reputation, as noted by Art Downs in *Wagon Road North: Historic Photos of 1863 of the Cariboo Gold Rush*:

> He always carried his robes and wore them wherever he held court, whether it be a tent, store, saloon, or cabin. He was called a hanging judge, but he never hanged a man the jury didn't convict, and hanging was the only legal penalty for murder. His drumhead justice was the law that American miners could understand; his fearlessness won the respect of all. He was willing to fight with fists or with lawbooks, and never relented. At Clinton he once sentenced a man and later in his hotel room heard the fellow's companions plotting to shoot him. The Judge listened for awhile, then emptied his chamber pot over them.
>
> Dr. Cheadle passed the Judge near Clinton on the Cariboo Wagon Road in 1863 and wrote: "Passed Judge Begbie on horseback. Everybody praises his just severity as the salvation of Cariboo and terror of rowdies."
>
> One miner summed him up thus: "Begbie was the biggest man, the smartest man, the best looking man, and the damndest man that ever came over the Cariboo Road."

Another lawman who gained a reputation for toughness was Peter O'Reilly. In April 1859, he was appointed a stipendiary magistrate and in the early 1860s was sent to Wild Horse Creek in the East Kootenays, scene of a gold rush that attracted several thousand miners, mostly from the United States. Here O'Reilly delivered an address that has become legendary.

Since there was no stenographer to record his words, there are many versions of what he said. Possibly the most accurate account is in a book called *Fifteen Years' Sport and Life in the Hunting Grounds of Western America and B.C.*, written by W.A. Baillie-Grohman, a sportsman-developer who arrived in the East Kootenay in 1882. According to Baillie-Grohman, when O'Reilly arrived at Wild Horse he addressed a group of miners in front of "the single-roomed cabin which he had turned into a temporary courthouse . . . Standing near the pole from which floated the Union Jack . . . he said: 'Boys, I am here to keep order and to administer the law. Those who don't want law and order can git, but those who stay with the camp, remember on what side of the line the camp is; for, boys, if there is shooting in Kootenay there will be hanging in Kootenay.'"

Only one flurry of gunplay erupted at Wild Horse, promptly settled in judicial style by 27-year-old magistrate and constable John C. Haynes. A month or two later, Colonial Secretary Arthur N. Birch visited the scene after 24 days in the saddle from Hope on the Fraser River. He reported: "I found the British Columbia mining laws in full force, all customs duties paid, no pistols to be seen and everything as quiet and orderly as it could possibly be in the most civilized district of the colony . . . much to the surprise and admiration of many who remembered the early days of the state of California."

The measure of the miner's regard for the four policemen ultimately stationed at Wild Horse was demonstrated when Constable John Lawson was killed there by a horse thief named Charlie "One Ear" Brown, who fled across the US border to apparent safety. A quartet of miners promptly pursued One Ear to the border but didn't bother with the formality of waiting for customs and immigration. They kept on going, caught him and shot him.

During the 92 years that the BC Provincial Police were the front line of law and order, they were always few in number. Even by 1900 there were only 100 men to police an area some 50 percent larger than France. They nevertheless maintained the peace and did it well, even though they occasionally bent the rules.

The work of these pioneer policemen is the theme of the chapters which follow. They functioned in a land once described by Canada's famed humorist Stephen Leacock as "an empire in itself"—albeit a rugged empire amidst a sea of snowcapped peaks. Some have dubbed it the land of exaggeration. "Extremes" is perhaps the better word. Among its offshore islands, tides can race up to 16 knots; in mountain passes winter snowfall can be 65 feet (19 metres) and temperatures can range from 43 to -57°C (109 to -72°F).

All of which emphasizes that the province's pioneer policemen had many discomforting days in the saddle, on snowshoes, travelling by dog teams, in canoes and river-boats, and on the wind-aroused waters of British Columbia's multi-thousand-mile coastline. There are many recorded instances of them bringing their prisoners by horse and canoe 1,000 miles (1,600 kilometres) to a courtroom. Then, in the 1890s, came launches with open naptha engines that were gradually replaced by a fleet of diesel-powered cruisers. Finally, the air age arrived, and some officers piloted planes.

As far back as January 1863, Chief Justice Matthew Baillie Begbie, in a plea to Governor James Douglas for increased police pay, had this to say of them:

> The fact is that most of the constables in the upper country are men who have hitherto filled superior stations in life; some of them having even held field officers' commissions in Her Majesty's army and most of them are provided with some small means of their own. But for this, it is an arithmetical certainty that they could not exist without running into debt, which would very much interfere with their utility. They are kept upright in their present position by the habit of discipline, by a sense of honor and by the hope of speedy promotion.

Even though over 30,000 heavily armed miners from the United States stampeded to the Fraser River in 1858, there was remarkably little lawlessness, despite the fact that miners outnumbered policemen by over 1,000 to 1. Hubert Howe Bancroft, the Pacific Northwest's foremost historian, observed, "Never in the pacification and settlement of any section of America have there been so few disturbances, so few crimes against life and property."

These tales of law enforcement are as factually correct as years of research can make them. But as they span a century, changes in jurisdiction and rank may occasionally be puzzling. For clearer understanding, a little background information is perhaps appropriate.

In 1858, the sudden influx of tens of thousands of gold seekers into the rocky canyons of the Fraser River transformed the fur-trading character of Britain's Pacific Coast colony into a copy of the 1849 stampede to California. To organize a constabulary in the newly proclaimed colony, Colonial Secretary Bulwer-Lytton dispatched 43-year-old Sub-Inspector Chartres Brew of the Royal Irish Constabulary. Immediately upon Brew's arrival on November 19, 1858, Governor Douglas appointed him chief inspector of police at a swearing-in ceremony at Fort Langley, on the Fraser River. Brew's handful of locally recruited policemen soon extended their activities to a new gold strike on Williams Creek in the Cariboo Country. Later, they were on hand when a fresh bonanza was uncovered at Wild Horse Creek in the southeast corner of the colony. Thereafter, whenever a miner found gold, a policeman was soon at his elbow.

In this fashion, the force penetrated into the wilds of the Omineca and, finally, the far-distant Cassiar and Stikine. By this time, British Columbia had become a

Canadian province, and Brew's colonial police were now known as provincial police. Fifteen years later, in 1874, the North West Mounted Police made their red serge the symbol of law and order on Canada's central plains. The BC police, however, had predated the Mounties by 16 years. In the course of time, the force was divided into 14 districts, each with a chief constable in charge. In each district, constables were in charge of detachments. This system lasted 66 years. In 1924, semi-military ranks and uniforms were introduced. Instead of keeping in contact with a multitude of districts, the superintendent (now ranked as commissioner) communicated only with inspectors commanding five divisions.

Finally, in 1950, an agreement was ratified between the province of British Columbia and the federal government whereby the Royal Canadian Mounted Police assumed responsibility for law enforcement. There is no question that the BC Provincial Police were held high in public esteem throughout their history. When absorbed into the RCMP in the summer of 1950, they were regarded by the federal force as a rather exceptional corps.

The far-ranging BC police officers saw the coming of the telegraph, the telephone and electric light and also were on duty when the four-horse stagecoach gave way to the train, the automobile and the airplane. They readily embraced anything new that would make them more efficient and were proud that their experiments enabled them to establish the first city-to-city short-wave police radio communication system in North America.

Whether assisting victims of fire or flood, escorting fugitives from foreign countries or merely performing the daily routine of urban duty, these British Columbia policemen did it with pride born of a sense of history. This book is a memorial to the men of the BC Provincial Police, who in 1858, with a quiet sense of duty, began to curb the lawless.

1

The Evidence of the Gold-Nugget Stick Pin

ON A SULTRY AFTERNOON IN early August 1866, Wellington Delaney Moses, Barkerville's black barber, beckoned the next customer to the chair. He was James Barry, one of the town gamblers, a tall, hard-faced Texan who slung his broad-brimmed felt hat on a peg and, with a curt nod of recognition, took his seat. Although they had met before, Barry, the southerner, was holding fast to his ingrained ideas about colour.

As Moses slipped the white sheet under Barry's chin, he suddenly paused. A gold-nugget stick pin on the gambler's black string tie held the barber's attention. Although the pause was only for a second, it started a sequence that 12 months later ended with Barry's death at the end of a rope.

It was late when Moses finally retired to his bedroom behind the barbershop. On this night, like many others, he found it hard to sleep, mainly because on the other side of the pitch-pine wall was Ross and Burdick's Dance Hall and Saloon. Long after midnight, through the rough siding, the hoot and stamp of miners and girls and the frenzied sawing of fiddlers invaded the room. Moses lay awake, thinking of Barry's nugget pin. It worried him because in a vague sort of way he knew he'd seen it before. And then he remembered. The nugget pin belonged to Charles Blessing. He was sure of it. There couldn't be another like it.

Moses's association with Blessing had its origin in 1858, when gold was discovered on the gravel bars of the Fraser River. Upward of 30,000 men had stampeded northward from California and elsewhere, among them Wellington Moses. But instead of heading for the Fraser, Moses started Victoria's first barbershop. He also offered customers the luxury of a bath, despite the fact that water was a scarce commodity peddled from a horse-drawn barrel at 40 buckets for a dollar.

The subsequent Cariboo mining boom of the middle 1860s made Barkerville the biggest town in the Canadian west and pulled Moses in that direction. He opened a shop in Barkerville. It must have been profitable since he followed the custom of the affluent by wintering in Victoria when the Cariboo's long winter closed down mining. In the spring of 1866, on the journey back to Barkerville,

Moses met Charles Morgan Blessing at Yale. As they were both heading in the same direction, they decided to travel together as "chummies," in the language of the day.

Blessing was 30, the scion of a wealthy New England family. He had followed the wanderlust for gold, first to California, then British Columbia. Despite rubbing shoulders with the roughest of men, he had retained his gentlemanly manner. As a northerner, he had more liberal views toward colour and apparently found in Moses an independence of mind that few New Englanders had encountered.

The two travelled the Cariboo Road in one of Barnard's six-horse stages, up through the sagebrush country to Soda Creek, from where they caught the sternwheeler to Quesnel, arriving about 7 P.M. on May 28. Since accommodation was scarce, they went to bed "in the custom of the country," which meant rolling out their blankets on Brown and Gillis's saloon floor in the company of other tired travellers. At the end of the room, the bar stayed open, the sleepers oblivious to the noise.

The next afternoon, Moses and his friend fell in with James Barry, or rather Barry seemed to fall into their company. Slick and debonair, it was plain to them that if Barry toiled with his hands, it wasn't in a mine. In answer to their questions, he conceded he had a natural bent for the intricacies of any card game involving money. Blessing suggested they adjourn for a drink. It was then that gambler Barry admitted that his card sense had lately gone awry. He was broke.

Blessing opened his wallet at the bar and drew out a 20-dollar Bank of British Columbia note, upon which Moses gave him the quiet tip to avoid spending too much. Blessing said with a grin, "I've got a few more of these before I'm broke." Neither apparently noticed the look of sudden interest on Barry's face.

After a few drinks, it was agreed that Blessing and Barry would start the next morning along the trail for Barkerville. Moses had decided to stay in Quesnel to find a man who owed him some money. Barry suggested that in order to avoid the crowded sleeping quarters in the saloon, he and Blessing bunk down in a nearby vacant shack. With a goodnight to Moses they moved off into the dark. The next morning, Moses sought out the shack, but they were gone. A Native man camped nearby said he'd seen them fold their blankets and head for the Barkerville wagon road at daylight.

When Moses arrived in Barkerville and looked around for Blessing, he ran into Barry coming out of Jimmy Loring's saloon. The gambler would have passed the barber had not Moses grabbed him by the arm to inquire about his friend. "Oh, that fellow," drawled Barry, as if he had a hard time recalling him. "He wasn't much good on the trail. Got sore feet or something and quit. I think he went back to Quesnel."

Weeks passed, and as Moses plied his scissors and razor he occasionally thought of Blessing and the nugget pin he had shown the barber on the way up from Yale. He often asked a newly arrived miner if he had heard of him, but nobody had. Barry, meantime, was here and there around Barkerville, Richfield and Camerontown. Though separately named, they were essentially one community linked by a long main street, distinguished not only for the size of the potholes but for the number and variety of saloons, most with dance hall and gambling facilities.

At night, in bedlam under the glare of naphtha lamps, each saloon proprietor did his best to separate the miners from their pokes. Added attractions were the "hurdies," buxom girls recruited mainly from Germany and Holland who invariably wore a red blouse, hoop skirt and a red bandana around their heads, the bow on top. Their day started about eight in the evening, when for a dollar a dance they were whirled off their feet by exuberant miners to the jigging tempo of fiddle and concertina. After each dance—about one whirl around the floor—the girls led their bearded and booted partners to the bar, where they got a commission on the drinks. Gambler Barry was at home in this scene, and his smooth approach made him a favorite with most of the girls. When he wasn't manipulating cards or dice, he was rated the Don Juan of the dance halls, a reputation that required an occasional visit to the barber.

When Moses remembered where he'd last seen the nugget pin, he realized that Barry might have had something to do with Blessing's non-appearance in Barkerville. Moses knew that Blessing thought a lot of the pin, and he certainly wouldn't have sold or given it away to a chance acquaintance of Barry's type. Besides, he didn't have to sell it, he had money. Money! It increased Moses's feeling that something had happened to his friend. True, Barry was adept at coming out on the right side of a card or dice game, or collecting a slice of the earnings of some infatuated hurdy. But how much money did he have when he arrived?

The next day, Moses locked his shop and began some discreet inquiries. Finally, he got the information he wanted. From Sam Wilcox, boardinghouse keeper, he learned that when Barry arrived in Barkerville in early June, he took a room at Wilcox's for $12 a week. Asked to pay in advance, the man who was broke at Quesnel on May 29 had a 20-dollar Bank of British Columbia bill on June 2. Back in his barbershop bedroom, Moses was undecided about telling his story to the BC Provincial Police at Richfield, about one mile away. Then he thought better of it. After all, it was only suspicion.

A few weeks passed, then in late September Moses was cutting the hair of Bill Fraser, one of the men who had landed in Victoria in 1858. He knew a lot of Moses's early-day Victoria customers, and Moses asked him if he'd ever run across a gambler called Barry. "That character! Why? You a friend of his?" Fraser responded.

Moses intimated he had an interest in Barry's background. By coincidence, Fraser once had travelled up from

New Westminster with Barry. He had concluded from remarks Barry made that the tall Texan had seen the interior of more than one jail. He also seemed to know the inside story of a few recent robberies. When Fraser asked him how, Barry admitted he'd heard about them from "a fellow who was in the chain gang with me at New Westminster."

Fraser had noted that Barry always wore a Colt six-gun and cartridge belt. The miner was interested in the gun because he had a friend in New Westminster who had just lost one. In fact, the friend had supplied Fraser with its serial number in case he ran across it. Once or twice on the trip, Fraser tried to steer the conversation to guns, hoping to get a chance to examine Barry's weapon, but the gambler never let it out of his possession. "Even slept with it under his pillow," Fraser remembered. Fraser parted company with his dubious companion at Quesnel. It was the same day that Barry had made his acquaintance with Moses and Blessing.

After hearing Fraser's story, the picture was clearer in the barber's mind. He decided it was time to go to the police. The next morning, in the log-built Richfield police station, Moses related his suspicions to Chief Constable W.H. Fitzgerald. The district head of the police listened gravely to the barber's tale. "A very interesting story, Moses," said Fitzgerald at the conclusion, "and I'll have someone look into it. Meanwhile if you hear anything more..."

At that moment, he was interrupted by the appearance of Constable John H. Sullivan. "Excuse me, Chief," Sullivan said, "but we've just had word from Bloody Edwards' place. They've found a body there. Looks like murder."

"Any identification?" asked Fitzgerald.

"Yes, a man called Blessing. Charles Morgan Blessing. Ever heard of him?" In the silence that followed, Fitzgerald shot a glance at the Barkerville barber, but Moses had turned to gaze out of the window.

The immediate police investigation showed that a miner, out shooting grouse near Edwards's stopping place at Beaver Pass, had been searching just off the road for a wounded bird. Well into the thicket, he almost stepped on what he thought was some clothing. It certainly was clothing, but it covered what was left of a man. A jacket pocket yielded a wallet, empty of money but bearing the name of Charles Morgan Blessing. Nearby was a tin cup with the initials "CMB" scratched on the bottom and at the dead man's feet a clasp knife bearing the same initials. A bullet hole in the back of his skull told the manner of Blessing's end.

As news of the find swept Barkerville, Fitzgerald instructed Sullivan to bring in Barry. But Barry had left very suddenly. A warrant was issued, and the constable had to decide whether to try to catch him at Quesnel or further south at Soda Creek. Sullivan chose the latter option and swung into the saddle for a ride of 120 miles (195 kilometres). When he reined in his sweated mount at the Soda Creek steamboat landing, he learned that Barry had got off the sternwheeler two days before and had promptly taken the six-horse stage to Yale.

Then the quick-witted Sullivan thought of a brand new Cariboo country innovation: the electric telegraph. The Collins Overland Company had only just strung the wire to Quesnel, and now, for the first time, Soda Creek, Yale and New Westminster were in instant communication. The Soda Creek operator tapped out the message that told the BC Provincial Police at Yale of Barry's flight—the first time the telegraph was used in the province to catch a criminal.

When Barnard's stage pulled into Yale 12 hours later, a police officer was waiting. Barry gave a false name, protesting loudly that the policeman had the wrong man. He ceased protesting when the cell door slammed behind him. Sullivan was instructed to return Barry to Richfield. During the journey, Barry tried to convey to his escort that he'd seen two or three Chinese on the trail after he had parted from Blessing near the Edwards's place. Maybe, he suggested, they had something to do with Blessing's death.

At Barkerville, following the information supplied by Moses, the police traced Blessing's nugget pin to a dance-hall girl, who said she had got it from Barry. When the gambler arrived at Richfield, Fitzgerald showed him the pin and asked if it was his.

"Sure it's mine," said Barry.

"Where did you get it?" asked the officer.

The sketch of the gold-nugget stick pin made by Chief Justice Begbie in his bench book during the 1867 trial. *THE SHOULDER STRAP*

"I bought it from a man in Victoria years ago. He went back to the States."

"Ever notice anything peculiar about it?" persisted the officer.

"No," was the nonchalant reply. "It's just a nugget pin."

"That'll be all for the present," said Fitzgerald, a trace of satisfaction in his tone.

In the summer of 1867, Barry was led into the little courtroom at Richfield to face Chief Justice Matthew Baillie Begbie. As the trial unfolded before a jury of hard-faced Cariboo miners, they heard the dovetailing evidence of Crown witnesses accounting for all Barry's movements at the end of May 1866. Finally, cattle drover Patrick Gannon came to the witness stand. Gannon said he'd seen Barry and Blessing eating breakfast together by a roadside fire near the Edwards's place, just a stone's throw from where the body was later found.

The biggest impression was created by the barber, Wellington Delaney Moses, who identified the nugget stick pin handed to him by prosecutor H.P. Walker. How did he know it was the property of the murdered man? Because, Moses pointed out, when you looked at it in a certain way you could see the profile of a man's face on one side of the nugget. It was the face on the nugget that he had momentarily seen as he swung the sheet into position under Barry's chin. For proof, the pin was passed for inspection by judge and jury. They could see the face. In fact, as he held it in his hand, Judge Begbie sketched the pin in his bench book. Moses had given Fitzgerald this telltale clue, and Barry, questioned by the police, had fallen into the trap.

The jury found him guilty. At five o'clock on the morning of August 8, 1866, a gang of men erected a scaffold in front of the Richfield courthouse. At seven o'clock, Barry was hanged, and by eight o'clock the scaffold was gone. It was not only a speedy execution, it was the first public one in Richfield.

Moses continued his Barkerville business for many years and eventually expanded into sales of men's and women's wear. Today his barbershop has been restored and is one of many historical exhibits that annually draw tens of thousands of visitors to historic Barkerville. The Barkerville barber died in 1890. He was buried in the Chinese cemetery, since the community's main cemetery was reserved for whites.

2

The Man Who Was Hanged by a Thread

THE PEACE RIVER DISTRICT OF northeastern British Columbia is a big and spacious country, producing oil, gas and wheat. The area attracted many people of different nationalities during the pioneer era of the 1920s and 1930s. Among these men and women were the Polish-born Babchuks, Joe and Anna, who took up a homestead between Fort St. John and the Beatton River in 1930. Newly married, they had lived in a tent that summer while Joe cut enough poles to build a small one-room log cabin.

The Babchuks settled in their new home in mid-August. Their belongings were few: a cheap iron bed and bedding; a stove, bucket and basin; a rough table and chairs and some shelving. When the couple moved into the house, the gable ends above the wall were open; Joe figured on finishing them when he had more time, although fate decreed otherwise.

Mike Skakum, a neighbour, noticed the open gables as he walked up to the cabin one afternoon in early September. Mike hadn't seen Joe or his wife for a week or two, but thought that since he was going to Fort St. John the next day, the newlyweds might want him to bring something back for them. He knocked at the door, but there was no answer. He knocked again. Hearing no sound, he tried to peer through a window, but Anna Babchuk's new scrim curtains blocked the view. Skakum turned his attention to the woodlot where Babchuk cut his firewood. There was no sign of life there.

Puzzled, he wondered if the pair might be ill. He climbed on a water barrel at the end of the house and hauled himself up to look over the open gable into the cabin. When his eyes became accustomed to the gloom, he could see the Babchuks in bed, a dirty canvas tarpaulin covering all but their heads. He yelled at them, but they paid no attention. Then he knew why. They were both dead. Horrified, Mike dropped to the ground, ran to his battered old truck and headed down the gravel road to Fort St. John and BC Provincial Police constable Joe Devlin.

"Two dead," thought Devlin, as he scribbled a few notes. "Maybe murder and suicide." Then he called District Sergeant George Hargreaves Greenwood at Pouce Coupe, 50 miles (80 kilometres) away. In a few hours, the two police officers were tramping across the stubble to the Babchuk cabin. After forcing the door, they discovered that the couple had been shot as they lay in bed. The signs indicated that the crime had occurred at least two weeks before. Nearby on a chair was an alarm clock, the hands stopped at 4:30.

Propped against a wall was a 30-30 rifle, with one fired shell still in the breech and two live ones in the magazine. From the dirt floor of the gloomy little cabin, Sergeant Greenwood retrieved another empty rifle shell. The two policemen noted that Anna Babchuk had lain down on the bed without her shoes but wearing lightweight riding breeches and a sweater. Babchuk was in his underwear; his light grey suit hung over a chair.

Dirty dishes in a tin basin suggested that three people had eaten a meal. Judging the distance of the fired rifle from the bodies, Greenwood deduced that he was dealing with murder and that the murderer had thrown the tarp over the bodies to allay the suspicions of anyone peering into the cabin. Greenwood continued a thorough search of the cabin. There was no money in Babchuk's clothing. In fact, there was no money in the cabin. A small wooden trunk attracted the officer's attention, but there was nothing much of interest in it except a package of letters, most of them written in Polish. One, however, was in English, from a Mrs. Dron of Beaverlodge, Alberta. It gave Mrs. Babchuk the neighbourhood gossip, but there was one remark that Greenwood paid particular attention to: "Wayslki is making some nasty threats and says he's going to kill you both, but you needn't pay any attention to a fellow like him."

It was obvious that something had occurred between the Babchuks and Wayslki in the northern Manitoba town of The Pas, some 300 miles (485 kilometres) northwest of Winnipeg. Mrs. Dron's comment was an interesting lead.

Greenwood notified by radio Divisional Inspector W.V.E. Spiller in Prince Rupert. Spiller left immediately for Pouce Coupe, although the Peace River area was so remote in the 1930s that he was a week getting there. In the interval, Sergeant Greenwood ordered an inquest, preserved the fatal bullets and generally busied himself trying to pick up the threads of the Babchuk's social life. He could not find any trace of a man called Wayslki in the Peace River.

He did, however, pick up some interesting information from a farmer named Hamilton. He had seen a heavy-set, dark man around the Babchuk cabin on several occasions in August. This information led police across the provincial boundary into Alberta and to the cabin of Mike Sowry at Hythe. Sowry told a reasonable story. He'd been very friendly with the Babchuks, he said, and worked for them during August. In fact, he had helped build the cabin. There were two other men working with him at the time, Sam Burtula and Pete Runka. It appeared that they had all worked at Babchuk's place until August 14 or 15, then left. Sowry was heading for the little community of Hudson's Hope, west of Fort St. John, when Hamilton saw him. At

Hudson's Hope, Sowry made a few purchases, then headed for his home at Hythe. He arrived there on August 21. He was sure of the date and remembered meeting Sam Burtula there and buying him a few drinks in the beer parlour.

While Greenwood and Devlin were in Alberta, they interviewed Anna Babchuk's correspondent, Mrs. Dron, at Beaverlodge. She said she had known the Babchuks at The Pas when Anna had been "going steady" with young Wayslki. Then she suddenly dropped him and married Joe Babchuk. Wayslki was furious at being jilted. In fact, he was the main reason for the newlyweds leaving Manitoba for the Peace River.

When Inspector Spiller finally arrived at Pouce Coupe and learned of Devlin's enquires, he promptly dispatched a radiogram to headquarters in Victoria suggesting a plain-clothes man be sent to check on Wayslki at The Pas. "Tell him to travel by way of Edmonton and I'll meet him there," the inspector requested.

The man picked was Detective Sergeant W.A. "Bill" MacBrayne, a South African and First World War veteran who had been a policeman in western Canada for 30 years. Tall and soldierly, MacBrayne had a unique record in the BC Provincial Police for solving tough problems. He was briefed on the Peace River killing, then set off for northern Manitoba. He soon found Wayslki—a husky young Ukrainian—working as a section hand on the Hudson's Bay Railway. Wayslki was still bitter about his treatment by the fickle Anna Babchuk, but MacBrayne's close check showed he had not been away from Manitoba for the past 12 months.

While MacBrayne was busy in Manitoba, Sergeant Greenwood had found another of Babchuk's friends—Tom Boichuk, a middle-aged man. He said that on August 16 there had been a get-together at Pete Runka's place, a sort of housewarming for the Babchuks, who were present with Boichuk, Mike Sowry and Sam Burtula. During the party, Babchuk asked Boichuk to pick up his mail the next time he went into Fort St. John. It was August 22 when Boichuk went there, but there was no mail. He called on the Babchuks to tell them, but they didn't answer his knock.

Through a chink in the logs he could see a corner of the tarpaulin over the bed and the clock on the chair. "The hands," said Boichuk, "were at 2:15 and the clock must have been going because I checked my watch, and it was the right time."

Boichuk's account narrowed the date of the murder. The police checked Burtula for his version of the housewarming. He confirmed Boichuk's story and remembered Boichuk offering to bring back the Babchuk mail. And he was sure of the date—August 16. Did he meet Mike Sowry after that date? Yes, he met Sowry in the beer parlour at Hythe. Mike seemed to have quite a roll of bills and bought a round for everyone. He said he'd just come into town. The date was August 23.

"How are you so sure of the date?" asked Greenwood.

For answer, Burtula produced his bank book and pointed to a deposit made that day. The mystery was deepening. Sowry had claimed he'd returned to Hythe on August 21. By this time, Detective Sergeant MacBrayne had arrived in the Peace River from his Manitoba investigation and quickly noticed a discrepancy in the date of Sowry's homecoming. The Babchuks were alive on August 16 at Burtula's party, but they could have been dead on August 22 when Boichuk said the alarm clock was running. How long had they been dead? And how long would an alarm clock run?

The police checked back with rancher Hamilton and described Mike Sowry. Yes, that was the man he'd seen around the Babchuks. Hamilton had last seen him on the afternoon of August 21. The police now realized that Sowry wanted to put himself at Hythe on August 21. He was moving his dates back, but the evidence was against him. Then Constable Devlin learned that no one around Hudson's Hope had seen Mike Sowry around the middle of August. Furthermore, the storekeeper denied selling him anything.

In the meantime, Detective Sergeant MacBrayne had experimented with the Babchuk alarm clock and learned that it ran down in 36 hours. If it was running on the afternoon of August 22, then the Babchuks were killed on August 20 or 21. Was this why Sowry wanted to slow down the calendar? Maybe. In any case, it was a purposeful Spiller and MacBrayne who left for Hythe that afternoon to further question Mike Sowry.

Sowry met them at the door with an inquiring look. He was wearing a black work shirt and dark tie, which contrasted with his light grey suit. MacBrayne thought there was something oddly familiar about that suit. He had seen one like it quite recently, but couldn't remember where.

Sowry's wife listened as the police investigators asked him to repeat his movements in mid-August. Sowry related how he had been looking for a homestead and had driven to Pouce Coupe and left his car there. Then he walked by stages to Fort St. John, met the Babchuks and worked as their helper until August 15. He attended Burtula's party on August 16, then went on to Hudson's Hope, sleeping in the bush for two or three nights on the way. After that, he headed back home and got to Hythe on August 21.

"Burtula," interposed MacBrayne, "says you were in the Hythe beer parlour on August 23."

"He's mistaken," said Sowry.

"He says you had quite a roll of bills. Where did you get the money?"

"I only had a dollar or two," said the uneasy suspect.

MacBrayne suddenly turned to Mrs. Sowry. "When did your husband get back to Hythe?"

"I wasn't here," replied Mrs. Sowry. "I was visiting friends in Beaverlodge."

"Did he give you any money when you got back?" went on MacBrayne.

"Yes, fifty . . ." she blurted out.

"Fifty what?"

"Fifty dollars." It was almost a whisper.

MacBrayne turned to Sowry. "Where did you get the money, Sowry?"

"I got it from two men," came the halting answer. "Two men I drove from Pouce Coupe to Fort St. John."

"You said you left your car at Pouce Coupe and walked." There was silence. Inspector Spiller rose. "Better get your hat, Sowry, you're coming with us."

Before the trio departed in the police car, MacBrayne made a quick check of Sowry's car. The glove compartment yielded a box of 30-30 cartridges. There were four shells missing, and they were the same brand as the empties found at the murder scene. But still the detective sergeant wasn't satisfied. There still was the matter of the ownership of the rifle. Sowry denied it was his, and Babchuk couldn't talk.

Although the investigation had narrowed the time of the murder to within 24 hours, the policemen still hadn't discovered the identity of the mysterious visitor who had shared the Babcock's last meal. And there was still no clue as to how much money had been in the cabin. As the police officers drove back to Fort St. John with the murder suspect, something else kept disturbing MacBrayne—something to do with the suit Sowry wore.

Only when they stepped inside the Fort St. John police office did MacBrayne remember why Sowry's suit looked familiar. It was the same sort of grey suit that the murdered

Babchuk had worn. In fact, it was almost identical. In the police office, MacBrayne went casually to the cupboard where the Babchuk exhibits were held. He took out the dead man's coat and pants and studied them closely with a magnifying glass. He took the pants over to the window for a closer look. Suddenly he turned to Sowry. "Take off your coat, Mike, I want to look at it."

Bewildered, Sowry did as he was told. MacBrayne studied the coat in silence, the only sound the ticking of the office clock, then tossed it on the table.

"You can lock him up, Joe," he said to Devlin, "and then bring me his pants."

With Sowry gone, Greenwood and Spiller waited for an explanation. "Ever hear of a man who went into a restaurant and came out with the wrong hat?" The two nodded. "Well," went on MacBrayne, "you've just seen the man who picked up the wrong coat at the scene of a murder."

"You mean . . .?" said Greenwood.

"Sure. Sowry is wearing Babchuk's coat. And Sowry's coat is in the exhibit cupboard. They look the same, but Babchuk's suit has a dark thread in it."

At the trial, a ballistics expert testified that the gun found in the Babchuk cabin fired the fatal bullets and the shells came from the box in Sowry's possession. Sowry had no money prior to August 21, but he displayed a roll of bills in the Hythe beer parlour and gave his wife $50 when he got home. Apart from his false statements to the police, the most telling piece of evidence was the mix-up in the two grey suits. In his haste to get away after the murder, Sowry, in the dim light of the cabin, had grabbed the wrong coat and left his own in its place.

Reconstructing the crime, the Crown contended that the Babchuks had offered Sowry a meal and a bed on the floor for the night. Mrs. Babchuk, not wanting to undress in front of Sowry, took off her shoes and lay on the bed fully dressed. When Sowry was sure they were asleep, he shot them, took the money and his coat and fled into the night.

When Mike Sowry climbed onto a platform at Oakalla Prison a few minutes before seven o'clock on the morning of August 14, 1931, Canada's official executioner might have thought he was adjusting an ordinary rope around the doomed man's neck. But the policemen who had solved the murder knew that the real rope was made of thread—the thin, dark thread from a murdered man's coat.

3

Terror at Taylor's Camp

JACK MYERS WAS TOUGH, no doubt about that. Tough with his tongue, with his boots, with his fists and especially tough with a gun in his hand. Despite his lawless outlook on life, whether sailing into a southeaster, climbing a mountain or knocking a man down, he did it all with equal facility. Sometimes, but not often, he met his match among the axe-swinging fraternity in caulk boots, woollen shirts and stagged-off denims who logged British Columbia's coastal forests a century ago. They were men who toppled 20-storey-high Douglas firs and skidded them in sections to tidewater with bull teams.

There were five such men with Jack Myers in the log bunkhouse of Taylor's camp on Read Island at the northern end of the Strait of Georgia when trouble started that Sunday night of June 25, 1893. It began when trigger-quick Myers offended "Big Jack" O'Connor, who reacted by yanking a loaded Winchester rifle from the wall. That was the cue for the catlike Myers to knock the rifle from O'Connor's hands and stick the muzzle of a .44 Colt in his belly. The impact threw O'Connor into a chair, but he grabbed the revolver barrel as he fell and twisted it sideways before it fired a death-dealing slug.

Bob Burns leaped from his bunk to separate the struggling pair and grasped the revolver across the frame. Three hands strove for the long-barrelled Colt. "Don't shoot, Jack," O'Connor cried as the table and lamp crashed to the floor. Then came the revolver's thunderous report and O'Connor fell back with a groan, a bullet in his chest. The other bunkhouse inmates, who'd all been drinking, were startled into action by the gunshot. One grabbed the lamp from the floor and relit it to look at O'Connor's wound. An hour later, he was dead.

The man who fired the gun, Jack Myers, was a man with no conscience. He had been in the United States and boasted of killing four men. He had also been jailed for stealing logs and later earned another sentence for forgery in Everett, Washington. From there, he managed to saw his way to freedom, but Washington became a little too hot when the local sheriff posted a reward of $100 for his capture, so Myers crossed the border into British Columbia.

In June 1893, Myers landed on Tumbo Island, one of Canada's Southern Gulf Islands, to complete a deal for a small black and green sailboat. He sailed it across the strait to Burrard Inlet at Vancouver. After a few discreet inquires, he found on the inlet's north shore a man with whisky for sale. Myers bought 10 cases of "Gaelic" whisky and a case of champagne and headed up the strait to begin business as a bootlegger. His destination was the upper end of the strait where, in an indescribable tangle of fjords and channels, it could be said, "There ain't no Ten Commandments, only men with a thirst." Here the waterways ranged from the broad sweep of a wide channel, slicked here and there with eddies and boilers, to hole-in-the-wall gaps between islands where the muffled roar of the tide-race echoed from skyscraping cliffs.

The night before the shooting, Myers had dropped anchor in Whitestone Bay, at the northwest end of Read Island. Scenting some business, he strolled up the trail to Taylor's camp. In the bunkhouse, he found a friend, faller Jack O'Connor. With a friendly grin, O'Connor extended his hand. "What are you doing away up here, Myers?"

"I don't use that name anymore," was Myers's quiet warning. "Call me Ben. Ben Kennedy." So it was as Ben Kennedy that O'Connor introduced the tough little stranger to the crew—old Salem Hinkley, Angus Cameron, Jack O'Neill and Bob Burns. Myers had the forethought to bring a bottle from his stock. After it had circulated, he revealed that he had more—at $2 a bottle. The loggers bought, drank, argued and finally slept. Myers returned to his boat.

The next morning, someone suggested going out to get a deer. More whisky appeared, and eventually O'Connor and Burns set off with Myers in his boat. The expedition produced more drinking than hunting, for the loggers soon came staggering back empty-handed. Burns, they gleefully reported, had fallen overboard and had to be retrieved with a boathook.

In the bunkhouse, Hinkley and the others played cards and drank, and by the evening they were snoring in their bunks. Myers had drunk less than the rest, but late that evening he and O'Connor got into a heated discussion about the merits of Myers's terrier. "Best bloody watchdog in the country," was Myers's opinion. "Put him to guard something and he never moves."

"I'll bet I'll make him move," was O'Connor's contention, which he backed with a five-dollar bill. Myers threw his coat on the floor, and the dog took up his position. O'Connor's solution was to urinate on the dog, which promptly moved. This so enraged Myers that he drew his .44 Colt and let fly at the dog as it fled for the open door. O'Connor suddenly yanked the Winchester from the wall. "Hey! Hold on there! You can't do that."

The next thing the logger knew, the rifle had spun from his hands and he faced the muzzle of Myers's six-gun. Burns interceded. Then came the fatal shot that killed O'Connor.

Unconcerned, Myers went back to his boat and turned in. The following morning, he returned to the bunkhouse to talk things over. He proposed reporting the matter to the provincial police, saying that O'Connor had committed suicide. If the others stuck to the story, he figured all would be well. But the loggers caught the idea that Myers would have a gun in his pocket during the interrogation. The proposal received a sullen reception, and Myers realized he wouldn't get any co-operation in his wild scheme. It was probably this attitude of brooding resentment that encouraged Myers to discreetly pick up the Winchester and a shotgun and take them down to his boat. From then on, a cat-and-mouse game went on between Myers and the loggers. Once, for a test, he left his revolver on a bunk while he went over to the stove and made himself some coffee.

"All right, Kennedy, we've got you now!" came a sudden, taunting command. Myers whipped round to size up Burns with the .44 in his fist.

"What are you going to do?" asked Myers, advancing toward the gun muzzle.

"Going to tie you up and take you to Comox and hand you over to the police."

"You forgot something," said Myers. "There are no shells in that gun." Before Burns could check, a lightning punch caught him on the jaw and the gun dropped to the floor.

Monday and Tuesday passed in an uneasy stalemate, with O'Connor's body lying in a nearby shed. Finally, on

Wednesday morning, the men discovered that Burns had left quietly during the night in a skiff. He was on his way to Cortes Island to inform Justice of the Peace Mike Manson of the killing. Burns's action broke the deadlock. Myers hauled up his anchor and sailed out of the bay. The four loggers watched the bootlegger's black-hulled sloop head toward Whitestone Pass.

A few days later, coroner and Justice of the Peace Manson, with Constable W.B. Anderson of Comox, landed at Read Island to hear the loggers' story, corroborated by the bullet hole in the floor. As he pieced the evidence together, Anderson figured the loggers had consumed 16 bottles of whisky in 24 hours. He noted, too, that Myers had an unusual number of firearms with him: a .38 and a .44 Colt revolver, a .44 Winchester rifle, a shotgun and a .50-calibre Express rifle.

Constable Anderson set out in search of the fugitive. Two days later, as he approached the shoreline of Ramsay Arm, he was challenged by the thunderous report of the Express rifle. He returned the fire and ordered Myers to throw down his gun. Myers replied with two more shots from the bullgun, causing Anderson to duck for cover. Undeterred, the policeman reconnoitered the rear of Myers's hideout, then broke in the door of the cabin. It was empty. Myers had left a couple of empty bottles, Gaelic brand, and some firearms and ammunition. But the .44 Colt and the .44 Winchester were gone. The reason was obvious.

Myers had taken to the bush with two guns that used the same ammunition.

By now, the veteran Anderson had decided that this manhunt was going to be more than a one-man job. He returned to Comox to telegraph his district chief at Nanaimo, who reported events to headquarters in Victoria. As a consequence, the July stillness of Ramsay Arm was disturbed by the whistle of the little coastal freighter *Estelle*. On deck, scanning the shoreline through field glasses, was Superintendent Frederick S. Hussey, accompanied by the chief constable from Nanaimo and two constables. As part of Hussey's plan, the police were searching for any boats or canoes that Myers might steal to escape.

As they viewed the heavily timbered mountain slope that flanked Ramsay Arm, the police considered Myers was still on the west side of the arm. If he spotted *Estelle* there was a chance he might attempt to climb the 4,000-foot (1,200-metre) hump of the Downie Range and come down into Bute Inlet. In this case, Myers would have the choice of rafting to Stewart Island or walking the foreshore to pick up a Native canoe. Hussey decided to put two men ashore to pick up his trail, while he and the remaining constable, A.F. McKinnon, cruised the Bute Inlet side of the Downie Range. Two thoughts were in Hussey's mind: Myers would have to eat, and he'd have to shoot to eat. In that silent vastness a shot would be heard for miles. Moreover, if he lit a fire, the smoke would be seen.

While these plans were being laid, Myers was heading through the bush, terrier at his heels, the Winchester over his shoulder and the Colt at his hip. It was tough going, angling uphill, under and over deadfalls, through head-high salal and avoiding the vicious spines of luxuriant devil's club. He made a fireless camp the first night, high above the shoreline of Ramsay Arm. He reached the summit by the third night. The fourth he spent beneath a tree below the summit on the Bute Inlet side.

By now, Myers was gaunt, trembling with exhaustion and hunger. Rather than risk the noise of a shot, he callously killed his dog with a blow on the head. But if he couldn't risk a shot, he had to risk a fire. Aboard *Estelle*, far out in Bute Inlet, Hussey quickly saw the faint blue wisp of smoke that hovered above the trees. It meant only one thing: Myers was on his way down. "We'll meet him on the trail," Hussey said to McKinnon. Minutes later, the pair jumped into one of *Estelle*'s boats and rowed to shore.

Myers, meanwhile, slung some chunks of half-cooked dog meat over his shoulder and headed downhill. By sunset, he was only a short distance from shore and lay under a tree for another fireless night.

The next morning, the two police officers continued their uphill progress, closing the gap between them and Myers. Suddenly, Hussey, who was leading, halted and pointed to a stand of hemlock. Standing in the dappled morning light was Myers, rifle in hand, leaning against a tree and looking the other way. He appeared to be listening, as if some sixth sense told him he was not alone. There was irony in Myers's situation, for the dog who should have given warning was dead. The animal that had unwittingly provoked murder in his master's heart was now, by its absence, helping to put Myers into police hands.

Less than 100 yards (90 metres) separated Hussey and McKinnon from their quarry. They silently concealed themselves behind a tree as Myers trudged past them down the slope. He'd gone only half a dozen steps when Hussey's "Drop your gun and get your hands up!" startled the killer to an abrupt halt. The Winchester fell to the ground as his hands went skyward, and he turned to the men who had outsmarted him.

Myers was soon handcuffed and aboard *Estelle*. After picking up the two remaining officers, the little steamer headed for Comox. There, on July 12, Myers was charged with the murder of Jack O'Connor. Four and a half months later, he appeared before Mr. Justice Norman Boles in New Westminster. His defence lawyers were two bright young men: Charles Wilson and Edgar A. Magee. Attorney General Theodore Davie, assisted by Deputy Attorney General A.G. Smith, acted for the prosecution.

The jury heard the story of the drunken night at lonely Taylor's camp and how Myers had attempted to make the bunkhouse crew support the suicide theory. Bob Burns, who had gone for help, was not present to give evidence.

Tragically, he had drowned that August, but his deposition given at the preliminary hearing was admitted as evidence.

The defence's main point was that in struggling with the gun either O'Connor or Burns had caused its accidental discharge. They argued that since the gun was a single-action Colt, Myers's grip on the trigger could not have cocked the gun, and an uncocked gun could not be discharged. In any event, claimed the defence, five men drinking 16 bottles of whisky in 24 hours could not be relied upon to describe what did happen, especially when the shooting took place in complete darkness.

To the defence contention about the gun, Theodore Davie said, "There is no one present in this court who will disagree with the fact that the gun was discharged because the hammer fell on the cartridge." He let this reasonable assumption sink in before adding, "And the hammer fell on the cartridge because Myers fanned it with his left hand." It was an effective way of correlating the direct evidence that Myers was adept in the handling of firearms and familiar with the western technique of fanning the hammer of a single-action Colt. "It was that swift glancing blow with the heel of his left hand," continued Davie, "that cocked and released the hammer in one instantaneous movement and with sufficient leverage to break Burns's grasp on the cylinder." He followed his argument with a convincing demonstration.

The jury was out just over an hour and brought in a

verdict of guilty of manslaughter. Judge Boles sentenced Myers to life imprisonment.

The following year, two incidents occurred that reminded the provincial police of the drama-packed quest for Jack Myers. In the spring, the steamer *Estelle* blew up off Cape Mudge in a shattering explosion that killed the captain and every crew member. Only floating timbers were found to mark the tragedy. Later in the fall, in the penitentiary at New Westminster, Jack Myers took advantage of a guard's momentary preoccupation to bolt for freedom from a work gang. Disregarding the warning to halt, he was all but through an open gate when a guard's rifle cracked. Myers stumbled and fell. When they picked him up, he was dead.

4

Murder on the Trail of '98

BRITISH COLUMBIA'S PROVINCIAL POLICEMEN were spread so thin that often one or two were responsible for policing an area larger than many European countries. In addition, they were frequently totally isolated, without a road or even a telegraph line. In the records of the force, there are many instances of policemen using ingenuity to overcome problems resulting from isolation and the corresponding lack of a doctor, coroner, preacher, jury, undertaker and even a hangman. A good example of these problems—and solutions—is the case of Joseph Camille Claus, a stockily built man who had greed in his heart and murder on his mind.

I got the eyewitness account of Claus's downfall from the late William Howard Bullock-Webster. Though then in law practice in Victoria, he had been a member of the BC Provincial Police years before. Bullock-Webster was of a type not uncommon in the early days of the force. Son of an Indian army officer, educated at 400-year-old Sherborne School in England, he came to British Columbia in 1886. Six years later, he joined the BC Provincial Police, and when the 1897 Klondike gold rush demanded extra policing in the province's north, he was posted to the Cassiar country adjoining the Yukon border.

As chief constable, his district headquarters were at Glenora, not far from Telegraph Creek on the Stikine River. There were 11 men in his command, holding down detachments at Lake Bennett, Teslin Lake, Echo Cove, Fort Simpson and Port Essington at the mouth of the Skeena River. In all, he was responsible for an area far larger than his home country of England. Worse, the only access to Glenora was by sternwheel steamer during the brief summer months. After that, it was by dog team and snowshoes through miles of wilderness.

In the spring of 1898, a six-man party of gold seekers was checked through Glenora, heading for the Yukon. In the group were Joseph Claus, three Vipond brothers from Nanaimo, a Norwegian called Jens Hendricksen and a Scot aptly named Robert Burns. Hendricksen and Burns, in Western parlance, were "pretty well-heeled," with about $1,000 on them. The others, like most of the men stampeding north, had barely enough to live on. All, however,

These three men camped at Glenora in May 1898 were typical of the 30,000 who stampeded to the Klondike. HENRY JOSEPH WOODSIDE, LIBRARY AND ARCHIVES CANADA PA 016080

seemed to be travelling in harmony, and after a stopover of a day or so moved northward toward the frostbitten Eldorado on the far-off Yukon River. Some time later, word came back to Glenora that friction had developed in the party and it had split up, the Viponds deciding to go on alone.

Still later, a packer brought word of finding a derelict, snow-laden tent about 30 miles (48 kilometres) from Glenora. This news required police attention, so Bullock-Webster and Constable Malcolm McLean set off to investigate. Eventually, they found the sagging tent and discovered two men who seemed to be asleep. Closer examination, however, showed it was a sleep from which neither would awaken. The men proved to be Hendricksen and Burns, the former shot through the head, the latter the victim of ghastly head injuries probably caused by an axe. Their pockets were empty, which led Bullock-Webster to consider robbery as the most likely motive.

In his methodical style, the chief constable searched for a rifle and an axe. He found neither. Then, along a nearby frozen tributary of the Stikine, he noticed a blowhole in the ice. Underneath was a dark shadow. It was chilly work delving under the ice, but finally Bullock-Webster retrieved a bundle that turned out to be a rifle wrapped in a mackinaw coat. The killer had been smart enough to dispose of the rifle rather than have it found in his possession.

What puzzled Bullock-Webster was the fact that if the party had been reduced to three, where was Claus? Lured elsewhere and murdered like his partners? Were the Viponds responsible, and if so, where were they? These questions had to be put aside, however, as the police officers tediously sledded the bodies back to Glenora. Then came the task of thawing them out between two roaring fires. Afterwards, Bullock-Webster reluctantly undertook post mortems. Undigested stomach contents revealed that both men had eaten a meal two or three hours before they were killed. It was probably an evening meal, for the tent was up and they were in their blankets.

In the course of his examination, Bullock-Webster probed the bullet from Hendricksen. With the aid of miner's scales and comparison with other unfired bullets, he calculated that the lethal slug came from the rifle hidden under the ice. Though the ballistics test was rough and ready, he could say that the bullet was of matching weight and calibre.

With the medical part of the inquiry finished, Bullock-Webster then became the coroner. Empanelling a jury of miners, he laid the facts before them. The seasoned sourdoughs were unanimous in their verdict: "Murder by a person or persons unknown." The inquest over, the chief constable became undertaker, finishing his busy day by conducting a burial service. Then he reverted to his policeman's role of manhunter.

In due course, the Viponds were intercepted and questioned. It was apparent they knew nothing of the murders and possessed nothing belonging to the murdered men. But they did add some information. After the party left Glenora, Claus started questioning everything they did. For this reason, the Viponds went their own way in disgust.

This scrap of information intrigued Bullock-Webster. Maybe Claus wanted the Viponds out of the way. He could handle two men in a stealthy attack but not five. Bullock-Webster immediately sent word over the Yukon Telegraph Line to pick Claus up. Some time later, Claus mushed into Teslin Lake and right into the arms of Provincial Constable Arthur D. Drummond. Claus, who had been penniless at Glenora, was now found to have about $1,000 on him—in a purse that belonged to one of the dead men!

When asked about the money, he had an ingenious explanation, saying that one night Burns flew into a violent rage and shot Hendricksen. He then turned his rifle on Claus, who was just nimble enough to snatch up an axe and defend himself. Burns got the worst of it. After that, said Claus, he took their money for safekeeping and was going to hand it over to the first policeman he met.

When Claus was escorted back to Glenora, a few legal problems developed that threatened to prevent a trial. The Attorney-General's Department had arranged for Mr. Justice Walkem to go to Glenora, accompanied by Crown counsel and a lawyer for the defence. By a quirk in the immigration treaty between Britain and the United States, however, the legal party could not travel through Alaskan territory to British Columbia.

Meanwhile, Bullock-Webster had collected miners to act as jurors. They were not happy since they wanted to be on their claims for the spring breakup. With the trial apparently delayed, they decided to leave. Bullock-Webster, however, quickly displayed the ingenuity—and law bending—often necessary in far-flung police outposts. He conjured up a batch of subpoenas, attached large red seals, then slapped a paper in the hands of each prospective juror. He warned them that if they left the settlement they would face a six-month jail term.

Bullock-Webster had even prepared for the possible final eventuality—Claus's conviction and hanging. Years later, he told me he had bought a rope from the Hudson's Bay Company and arranged to use their fur loft for the execution.

"Who on earth was going to hang him?" was my interested query.

"Oh," said Bullock-Webster in his quiet fashion, "I figured I would have to do it. After all, I performed all other functions."

He was spared the possibility of this duty when word arrived that there would be no assize in Glenora. In addition to the immigration problem, there were an insufficient number of registered voters in the Cassiar, and no jury could be empanelled. Claus would be tried in Nanaimo. The miners "subpoenaed" by Bullock-Webster happily scattered to their claims.

In late June 1898, a jury of Nanaimo businessmen and coal miners listened with rapt attention to a story of murder and robbery in the frozen wasteland that bordered the mighty Stikine River. Claus was found guilty and sentenced to hang on August 14. On the eve of his execution, a guard noticed Claus acting strangely in his cell, but by the time help arrived, the prisoner was in a coma. Apparently he had taken some deadly poison, although where he got it remained a mystery. Some thought he had brought it with him from the North, secreted in the lining of his coat or the cuff of his pants. Others felt it might have been between the pages of a Bible his wife gave him the day before. Whatever the answer, it was the last act in one of the many tragedies that marked the Trail of '98.

CHAPTER

5

Hijack Route
to the Hangman

DURING THE 1920–33 PROHIBITION era in the United States, liquor smuggling from Canada, where the sale of liquor was legal, grew into an incredibly profitable venture. Not only were individuals involved, but also gangs controlled by criminals like the notorious killer Al Capone, whose illegal activities in 1927 alone earned him an estimated $107 million. Stemming from this booze bonanza were thousands of murders, since gang warfare was common and hired killers cheap. But these killings weren't restricted to gangs. Lesser hoods could be equally ruthless, as demonstrated by Baker and Sowash in the waters off southern Vancouver Island.

Owen W. Baker was tall and gangly, with an Adam's apple that moved convulsively in his scrawny throat. A lock of hair falling over his forehead gave him a folksy look that belied the savagery he later revealed. Harry "Si" Sowash was somewhat younger, and with his crewcut, broad shoulders and rugged build, he could have been taken for a university football player. In keeping with this academic impression, he read a lot and knew his way around in Greek and Roman history. He also had a sense of humour. After dictating and signing a lengthy murder confession, he passed it to BC Provincial Police inspector Tom Parsons with the remark, "A good caption for that would be 'The Toilers of the Sea.'"

I remember, as the pair awaited their execution, that Baker wrote to all his relatives and acquaintances pleading for money and legal assistance for a last-minute appeal. Sowash, on the other hand, wrote only one letter, addressed to the manufacturers of a well-known brand of shaving cream. They had originated a new sales gimmick that consisted of a little chain to prevent the cap from going astray. Sowash wrote the company telling them how, for years, he had been troubled by the cap falling into the drain hole of the wash basin. In a satirical vein, he thanked them for this boon to shavers. Of course, the company could not have known that their correspondent had just two weeks to live.

Baker met Sowash while he was doing a five-year stretch for white slavery in McNeil Island Penitentiary in Washington. Sowash was serving two years for selling stolen airplane parts. They were released during the heyday of rum-running, and Baker promptly got involved. Equipping himself with a yachtsman's peaked cap, a blue blazer with double rows of brass buttons, a flashlight and a phony police badge, he intercepted "rummies" as they unloaded a speedboat in the dead of night along some lonely Puget Sound beach.

His shout, "United States Customs! Stay where you are!" was the cue for the rum-runners to flee, leaving their booze, which Baker "confiscated." But he was also adaptable, quickly changing his method of operation to suit circumstances. When a man with four cases of Scotch in the back of his car stopped for a traffic light in mid-town Tacoma, Baker drove up and flashed his badge. After he had handcuffed the unfortunate man to his steering wheel, he fled with the Scotch.

Baker soon learned, however, that the booze business could be hazardous. On one occasion in Seattle, he sold 10 cases of gin that proved to be water. Unfortunately for Baker, the purchaser, accompanied by a couple of grim-faced pals, accidentally ran into him on a Seattle street corner. Confronted with his duplicity, Baker simulated amazement. "You don't say!" he gasped. "Well, it just happens the guy who sold me that gin is around the corner. I'll go and get him."

Baker quickly retreated to the basement of the Commodore Hotel, where he burrowed his way into a sawdust pile used for the heating plant. His enraged customers dragged him out of his hideout half an hour later and escorted him upstairs to a fourth-storey room. Here they held him by the ankles over the window ledge until he gave assurance of immediate reimbursement. All of which gives some idea of the hazards of the bottle trade in the Roaring Twenties.

After this alarming episode, but obviously still intent on staying in the liquor business, however hazardous, Baker chartered a fishboat. Picking Sowash and a new man, Charlie Morris, as accomplices, he cruised the shoreline of southern Vancouver Island looking for liquor caches which he hoped to steal. After a week of cruising they hadn't found a drop.

Then, off Sooke Harbour, the trio spotted a big, slow-moving fish packer heading in the direction of Victoria. Baker's interest was aroused, and he soon learned that the packer was *Beryl G* out of Vancouver. But instead of fish, she was on a booze shuttle run, carrying 600 cases a trip from the rusty old British freighter *Comet*, anchored beyond the three-mile limit off Vancouver Island's west coast. The skipper and owner of the packer was Bill Gillis of Vancouver, who had on board his teenage son, Bill. *Beryl G* usually anchored in a cove on the east side of Sidney Island, not far from Victoria, where she disposed of her load to speedy American craft owned by Pete Marinoff of Tacoma. When her hold was empty, *Beryl G* chugged back to *Comet* for another load, at the going rate of $6 a case.

About a week later, in a room in the New England

Hotel on Victoria's Government Street, Baker outlined the intricacies of the old customs racket to Sowash and Morris. Once they were aboard *Beryl G*, a peaked cap and brass buttons would reduce Gillis and son to mere onlookers as their cargo was removed. The plan included hiring a Victoria fisherman and his boat, and the next night the trio embarked from the Cadboro Bay Yacht Club and headed for Sidney Island. Here, Baker and Sowash rowed over and boarded *Beryl G*, but the plan went awry, for Gillis appeared with a rifle. Baker promptly shot and killed him.

The unexpected sound of gunfire from *Beryl G* made the fisherman and Charlie Morris uneasy. Then, out of the gloom, came Baker, furiously rowing the skiff. He gave sharp instructions to the pair to bring the fishboat along-side and lash it to *Beryl G*. As the fishboat got close, they saw young Gillis being herded along the deck by Sowash, who suddenly struck down the youth from behind. "The cold-blooded murderers!" muttered Morris to the fisherman.

With Baker and Sowash in command, there was no time for argument. *Beryl G*'s anchor was hauled up, and as the fishboat towed the packer out of the bay, the two men discussed what they should do with the bodies. Baker's answer was to handcuff them together, lash them to *Beryl G*'s anchor and throw them overboard. Since they had far too much liquor to handle at one time, they cached it here and there along the shoreline, some of it below the low-water mark, to be retrieved later.

Finally, the bloody night's work done, the fisherman was forced to take Baker, Sowash and Morris to Anacortes in Washington. Then he returned to Victoria, stunned at the turn of events he had unwittingly been pressed into. He decided, unfortunately, to keep silent. The blood-stained and abandoned *Beryl G* was found idly drifting with the tide in Haro Strait. She was towed to Victoria, where provincial policemen boarded her. They began their investigation by analyzing the blood stains on the deck and discovering the owner's identity, his business and habits. In the pilothouse, a camera yielded a role of film which, after being developed, showed one of Marinoff's boats leaving *Beryl G*. Marinoff, in turn, was able to pinpoint the moment when one of his boats lifted the last load from the ill-fated craft.

In the weeks that followed, police combed the Victoria and Seattle waterfronts and learned that Baker and Sowash had hired a Seattle craft to look for liquor cached in the Canadian islands. The liquor had been sold, but through dogged police work the individual purchasers were found. The brands tallied with Gillis's cargo.

Then the unfortunate Victoria fisherman was found, and he finally told the whole story. Warrants were issued. The first man captured was Charlie Morris in Seattle. It took many months to locate the other two. Finally, Baker was found working on a dredge in New York harbour, and Sowash was rounded up in New Orleans. Both paid for their night's work on the gallows, while Charlie Morris got a life sentence.

Because of the efficiency of the BC Provincial Police and the gallows end of Baker and Sowash, hijackers avoided Canadian waters from then on. Finally, the 1933 repeal of Prohibition in the United States ended the lucrative trade of booze running. Al Capone, by the way, did not escape either. Although he had killed many men himself, nothing could be proved, and he was jailed on an income-tax evasion charge. But fate dealt him a harsher sentence. He died a lingering death from syphilis.

6

The Clue of the Kids
and the Candy

STEVE DREVENUK, A FERNIE MINER, discovered the body on Monday morning, February 10, 1936, about 4 miles (6.5 kilometres) from Fernie. It lay below the highway at a point where the Elk River swings toward the road. The temperature was below zero, and the early morning sun cast long blue shadows on the frozen, snow-covered landscape. Drevenuk at first thought the figure lying face down near the riverbank was a drunk. Then he decided to check, realizing that anyone, drunk or sober, who slept beside a river in sub-zero weather would soon be a corpse.

At that moment, he heard a car coming and flagged it down. He and the driver scrambled down the bank to discover that the body was already a corpse—and frozen stiff.

Minutes later, they were telling their story to Corporal D.A. McDonald of the Fernie detachment of the BC Provincial Police. At 47, McDonald was a husky, 24-year veteran on the force. After making arrangements with the undertaker and coroner, he accompanied Drevenuk to the scene. McDonald studied the area carefully. Before going down the bank, he stooped and picked up two pieces of paper—the crumpled remains of candy-bar wrappers. He also noticed two beer-bottle caps, which he pocketed.

Then, a few steps down the bank, McDonald picked up a cardboard disc about the size of a quarter. The printing on it showed it was a wad from a 16-gauge shotgun shell. At the river's edge, as he knelt beside the dead man, the coroner and undertaker arrived. The three men turned the body over. The man appeared to be about 35, with dark hair. There were spots of blood on his chin and a ragged hole where a shotgun charge had torn into his throat. Near him was a cheap brown cloth cap, six empty beer bottles, some beer caps and another shotgun wad. They could gain nothing from the footprints because local fishermen had trampled the snow. A search of the dead man's clothing revealed two government letters addressed to Mike Hudock of Michel, a small coal-mining town 25 miles (40 kilometres) from Fernie. The letters indicated Hudock had been a welfare recipient.

"Hudock?" thought McDonald as he picked up his office phone to report to District Sergeant Andy Fairbairn at Cranbrook. "That name sounds familiar."

Then he remembered that the previous afternoon a Canadian Pacific Railway (CPR) policeman had phoned to say he had two lost children on his hands. McDonald had driven over to the station to pick them up. The oldest, age nine, said his name was Sammy Hudock and he lived at Michel. The puzzled McDonald asked Sammy how he and his brother got to the CPR station.

"Vince took us there," was the cheery response.

"Vince who?"

"Vince Macchione. He knows my dad and mum. He took us to the station in his car and said he'd pick us up later, but he didn't come back."

At the sound of the name, McDonald recalled that he'd had previous contact with Vince Macchione—a section hand, he thought, who lived at Galloway, some 22 miles (35 kilometres) to the west. Leaving the children in the police station, McDonald walked up town in search of him. It was about 5:15 P.M. when he caught sight of Macchione driving a blue coupe. But before the police officer could flag him down, Macchione had turned left down a side street. McDonald followed until, opposite the Royal Hotel, Macchione pulled to the curb on the other side of the street.

As the police officer crossed the street, he noticed a woman emerge from a doorway and get into the coupe. McDonald had a talk with her. She was the mother of the lost children and was glad to hear they were safe. Macchione seemed glad, too. Apparently an old friend of the Hudocks, he had been delayed and got back to the railway station to find the kids gone. With smiles all round, he drove Mrs. Hudock and McDonald to the police station to pick up the children. After this explanation, Corporal McDonald considered the incident closed. But it was to remain closed only until the next day.

A few hours after Hudock's shot-riddled body was discovered, Sergeant Fairbairn arrived at the Fernie police office and listened to McDonald's story of death on the bank of the Elk River and the coincidence of meeting Mrs. Hudock and Macchione the day before. Here McDonald paused. Had Hudock been lying dead off the highway while he was speaking to Mrs. Hudock about her children yesterday afternoon? McDonald had already phoned the police constable at Natal and asked him to break the news to Mrs. Hudock. After that, he phoned the constable at Wardner, telling him to go over to Galloway and see what Macchione had to say.

Just after lunch, Macchione appeared at the Fernie office with Robert Evans, Mrs. Hudock's brother. "I'm sure sorry to hear about Mike," Macchione told McDonald. "He was one of my best friends. I was with him only yesterday afternoon."

As the conversation developed, it became apparent that Macchione had been seeing a lot of the Hudocks. The family, he said, had been having a rough time with Mike being on welfare. He'd given them a little money now and again.

Last Saturday night, he had bought them a week's supply of groceries, then taken the family to Fernie's Northern Hotel for dinner. On Sunday, Macchione drove the family into Fernie again, and Mike had left them to meet someone. That was the last they saw of him. "I figured," Macchione concluded, "he got tied up with some fellows in a hotel room, and would come home later."

That evening at the inquest, a coroner's jury rendered the verdict that Hudock had been killed by a charge of shot that entered his throat. It had been fired at close range and wasn't self-inflicted. It was murder.

McDonald's first problem was to find the person who last saw Hudock alive. Persistent inquiries, however, produced nothing. Sergeant Fairbairn was inclined to the "woman" angle and went to Michel to interview Annie Hudock. Her story was simple. She and her husband and two children had driven to Fernie on Sunday in Vince's car to buy bottled beer. They tried the Waldorf first, but the hotel hadn't any. Then they parked outside the Royal, and she and her husband went inside while Vince and the kids stayed in the car. The woman at the Royal said she had no bottled beer, but they could have beer by the glass.

"Go and tell Vince to leave the kids in the car and come on in," Mrs. Hudock had told her husband. Hudock went to the car, spoke to Macchione, and then, instead of returning to the hotel, walked slowly down the street. Vince followed with the car.

Mike Hudock was murdered near Fernie in February 1936. *THE SHOULDER STRAP*

"I thought it funny," said Mrs. Hudock, "because Vince had given us the money to buy the beer. I never saw Mike after that," she concluded sadly.

"What did you do then?" continued Fairbairn.

"Well," said Mrs. Hudock, "in maybe half an hour when

they didn't come back, I went out to look for them." She said she found Macchione parking his car across the street from the Royal Hotel. Just as she was asking where Mike and the kids had got to, Constable McDonald had walked over and told them the children were at the police station.

"Did Vince say where Mike went?" queried Fairbairn.

"Well, he said he was going to see some man and just walked off."

"And how did the children land at the CPR station?"

"Vince said the kids wanted to run around, so he dumped them off at the station and said he would pick them up later. Then he went looking for Mike, and I guess he was late in coming back."

In a way, it was a dovetailing story, although Fairbairn couldn't help wondering why Hudock hadn't returned to the hotel to drink his beer. What made him change his mind and walk down the street? And how, in a small town like Fernie, did Macchione lose track of him? It was curious, too, that Annie Hudock didn't seem to be unduly burdened with grief. But perhaps she was the type of person who allowed little room for displays of grief or affection.

Meanwhile, McDonald, intrigued by the Hudock-Macchione relationship, decided to have a talk with the dark-eyed Italian.

"You thought a lot of the Hudocks?" was his opening statement.

"I sure did—my best friends."

McDonald thought quickly. Suppose Macchione was attracted to Annie Hudock? Standing treat and buying groceries would be one way of capturing her affections. He'd try it. "I guess you didn't like to see Mrs. Hudock so poor. Is that why you bought the groceries?"

"I guess that's about it," admitted Macchione.

"Maybe," ventured McDonald, "you liked Annie a little better than Mike?"

"Yes, I guess I did."

"So, I guess you saw a lot of her," continued the corporal, "maybe sometimes when Mike wasn't around?"

"Sometimes," came the halting admission.

It wasn't much of a clue, but it might lead to a motive. Within an hour, McDonald was at Mrs. Hudock's home with more questions. One was a leading one: Had Vince Macchione ever shown her any marked affection? Yes, McDonald learned. In fact, Vince had wanted to marry her and once urged her to leave Mike and go with him to the United States. Sometimes he gave her money for dresses. Macchione and Annie Hudock had been more than good friends for a couple of years.

After comparing notes with McDonald, Fairbairn decided to act. Late that night, Vince Macchione was arrested at his Galloway home on a charge of murder. He was in bed when McDonald arrived and sat up by the light of an oil lamp as the policeman searched the room for a shotgun.

"You've got a gun here; where is it?" snapped McDonald.

"I haven't got a gun. I never owned one," vowed Macchione.

"This yours?" asked McDonald, going through the pockets of an overcoat hanging over a chair.

"Sure it is," said the little Italian.

"Did you wear it last Sunday?"

"Sure."

"Then why were you carrying these?" asked McDonald as he produced two 16-gauge shells.

"I never saw them before," said Macchione in a low, unconvincing tone.

On a shelf above the stove were two boxes of 16-gauge shells. "Why did you get these shells if you haven't got a gun?" probed McDonald relentlessly, as Macchione dressed.

"I don't know how they got there," was the answer. McDonald took him out to the lean-to garage and spent the next few minutes looking over a blue coupe. Under the front seat were two more 16-gauge shells.

"I guess you don't know anything about these shells?" remarked the cynical policeman.

"Never saw them before," was the routine answer.

Even with Macchione under lock and key, there were still gaps in the case. The absence of the murder weapon prompted Fairbairn to put gangs of men exploring the culverts along the highway, probing snowdrifts and searching the riverbank. Nothing was found. Men who had worked with Macchione on the section gang were interrogated.

"Sure, Vince owned a shotgun," said Fred Kalt. "He bought it mail order from Eaton's. He picked it out of the catalogue."

"I saw him with it lots of times," said Bill Lagoda. "It was about 16-gauge."

"I delivered it to him," added Leon Simmons.

A body, a motive, a weapon and a question: Could Macchione take his victim 4 miles (6.4 kilometres) out of town, shoot him and return so quickly? On a practice run, the officers found they could reach the scene in seven minutes if they drove 25 to 30 miles (40 to 48 kilometres) an hour. A fast driver could do it in three or four minutes. One piece of the puzzle was in place. Another was the shotgun wads at the scene. Then there were the beer bottles. They were labelled Fernie Brewing Company, but where did Macchione get them? And on a Sunday? McDonald canvassed the licensed hotels and beer parlours but met with negative replies until he talked to Joe Perri of the Central.

"Sure. Vince was in here Saturday," said Perri. "He paid a small bill and asked me to set aside six bottles of beer in a paper bag. Said he would pick 'em up Sunday."

"And did he?"

"Yep. Came in Sunday afternoon just after four o'clock and picked them up. Mike Hudock was with him."

Interesting, thought McDonald. Macchione knew that no bottled beer was going out of licensed premises in Fernie on a Sunday, so he made sure on Saturday that he'd have bottled beer for Sunday. It was solid evidence.

Now McDonald had to prove that Macchione's car and its two occupants were on the highway on Sunday afternoon. Word was spread that the police wanted to see anyone who had noticed a blue coupe on the Fernie highway on Sunday, February 9. Incredibly, four men appeared at the Fernie police station the next day. They were electrical workers who had driven to Fernie that Sunday from Elko. Four miles (6.4 kilometres) from Fernie they had seen a blue coupe parked on the right-hand side of the road near the river. There was nobody in the car, so they concluded the driver was fishing. They had not noticed the licence number.

Fairbairn, still working on his "woman" theory, checked with Annie Hudock to see if they had called on anyone on the way back to Michel that fatal Sunday night. He learned they had dropped in to see the Sowchuks at Hosmer. Mrs. Sowchuk remembered the visitors: Annie Hudock, Macchione and the two kids. They said they'd been to Fernie, then, unexpectedly, Mrs. Hudock started to cry. Julia Sowchuk followed her into the bedroom, put her arm around her and asked what the trouble was.

"Mike's dead," Annie Hudock moaned between sobs.

"You're crazy!" had been Mrs. Sowchuk's retort. "Mike probably went off with a bunch of fellows and got drunk."

Fairbairn's hunch about the "woman" angle suddenly

became overpowering. He quickly returned to Annie Hudock's house. What had she meant by that remark at Hosmer? She had said her husband was dead before his body was found.

"It was Vince who put the idea in my head," said the distraught woman. "When he got into the car in Fernie that night he leaned over to me in the front seat and whispered, 'He's dead.'"

When Fairbairn returned to Fernie with this ominous admission, McDonald was waiting to discuss a clue they had so far overlooked—the candy-bar wrappers. For Macchione, the consequence would be as devastating as Mrs. Hudock's remarks. In the police office, McDonald pointed out to Fairbairn that while the four electrical workers had seen a blue coupe on the highway, it might have been somebody else's car. But there were the two candy-bar wrappers he had picked up at the murder site. While they might have been thrown out of a passing car, two men stepping out of a car to drink beer wouldn't likely eat candy bars. But the children? The Hudock kids?

The officers immediately headed back to Michel. While their mother looked on, the police officers asked the children if Vince had bought them candy on Sunday. Yes, before they got to the railway station he bought them each a candy bar. What did they do with the wrappers? There was a pause while they considered. "We just threw them on the floor of the car," said the children, unaware they were helping to put a rope around the neck of their father's killer. They named the brand of candy; it matched the wrappers in the police office. They must have been scuffed out of the car by the men's feet, or blown out when the car door opened.

The investigation had caused the policemen many extra hours of duty and many sleepless nights. But there were also some exhausting hours ahead for the jurors at Macchione's trial, or rather, trials. For seldom in the history of British Columbia was a man tried for his life so many times.

The first trial was held at Cranbrook in May 1936. Macchione's defence was simple: "I went to look for Mike and couldn't find him." The jury found him guilty, and he was sentenced to hang in August. On appeal, however, he got a new trial, but 12 months later he again heard a jury say "guilty" and was sentenced to hang.

Another appeal was made, and a third trial was ordered, this time at Vernon in the spring of 1938. The jury could not agree, and a fourth trial began immediately. Again the jury could not agree. A fifth trial was ordered, but this time it was different. The deadlock was broken by a new Crown witness, Rudolph Smalik, who said that on the fatal Sunday he had been curling at the Fernie rink. At about 4:30 P.M., while driving out on the highway, he had passed Macchione in his blue coupe. Mike Hudock was sitting beside him. Smalik knew both men well, and he was sure of the time because he was on his way to a new job and didn't want to be late.

For the third time in his long duel with the law, Vince Macchione heard a jury foreman give the dreaded pronouncement. This time there was no reprieve. Early on the morning of October 26, 1938, Vince Macchione, the "good friend" of the Hudock family, stood on the scaffold at Oakalla Prison, then knew no more.

7

Tragedy Stalked
the Silver Trail

IT WASN'T BY CHANCE THAT in the summer of 1920, prospector and outdoorsman A.S. Williamson found himself at the entrance to an abandoned mine shaft on a mountain 8 miles (13 kilometres) south of Hope in the Fraser Valley. In the depths of the cavern, standing ankle deep in ice-cold seepage, he noted by the light of his flickering candle that miners had cut their names in a timber, names like "Frenchy," "McEvoy" and "Ned Atkins." For years, Williamson had been hearing scraps of gossip from Native people about a lost mine in the Hope Mountains, and that summer of 1920 he decided to look for it. He said nothing to anyone and took a rifle to give the impression he was going hunting.

After following the east bank of Silver Creek for several miles, he headed on an old trail up Eureka Creek. At one point he noticed an old horse corral and, near timberline, the remains of an ancient log cabin with a huge fireplace and an assay outfit. Higher and higher he climbed around the shoulders of Silver Peak, until he came to a narrow ravine and the remains of a blacksmith's shop. The bottom of the ravine was filled with hardened snow, but near an overhanging rock wall was a crevasse between the rock and snow. He climbed down and on hands and knees entered a tunnel. Cautiously moving forward, he felt some wooden tracks under the water and slowly followed them. They led to a wooden ore car with iron wheels. It seemed as good as new. Tools were scattered around as if men had just quit work moments before, and here and there candles were stuck in the lagging.

Although he didn't know it at the time, Williamson had rediscovered British Columbia's first quartz mine, the ill-fated Eureka (or Eureka-Victoria as it was later known), where nothing had been touched since 1875. There were other events connected with the mine and its original owners that Williamson also didn't know—how the mine brought nothing but tragedy to the five people first involved, including "Happy Tom" Schooley, who met the hangman, and pioneer BC sawmill owner Sewell Prescott "Sue" Moody, who drowned when *Pacific* foundered off Victoria with the loss of all on board—nearly 300 people.

The story had begun in Yale in the summer of 1868 when Peter Emery returned from a hunting trip in the mountains and showed his friend Tom Schooley a sample of silver ore he'd picked up. It was rich stuff—fabulously rich.

Schooley, a miner, knew ore. He'd crossed the American plains with a wagon train to become a forty-niner in California, then headed north to Victoria in 1858 for the Fraser River rush. He'd seen Yale spring from a simple trading post to a wild community of honky-tonks and saloons. Tall, dark and handsome, always distinguished by his white cowboy hat, Tom Schooley was the life of every gathering and for that reason was dubbed "Happy Tom." The rock Pete Emery offered him was an exciting find. Schooley gave Pete a rifle for it and made a coffin for Pete's wife, who had just died. The coffin was a portent of what was to follow.

Schooley climbed Silver Peak and promptly recognized the ore as one of the richest silver finds in the country. Instead of staking claims, however, he got a Crown grant to three lots, then went looking for partners. First, he interested George Deitz, an old buddy from the original Fraser River rush. Backed by Wells Fargo money, Deitz was now running a prosperous stage line between Yale and the Cariboo. Another Fraser River original who put up money was S.P. Moody, founder of the sawmill community of Moodyville on the north shore of Burrard Inlet. In Victoria, Schooley sparked Frank Garesche's interest. Garesche, a former Wells Fargo employee in San Francisco, was in business for himself running a private bank. The fourth man was Henry Forman, a one-time Victoria alderman, who would become Schooley's father-in-law.

With this backing, the Eureka Mining Company was formed, and soon 3,000 fifty-dollar shares were bought up. After Schooley's block of shares was sold, his status changed from ordinary miner to well-to-do promoter. Then, after a whirlwind courtship, he married the beautiful Ellen Forman.

Unfortunately, trouble arose shortly after their San Francisco honeymoon when Happy Tom surprisingly turned into Surly Tom. Some say he was insanely jealous of his wife, others say he suspected his father-in-law of having designs on his money. More likely, Schooley's bad business judgment was the cause. Tom started out as if he had all the money in the world, but his funds dwindled after a succession of unwise investments. He became increasingly surly and suspicious, seeking more and more consolation from the bottle. Finally, in January 1874, when he and his wife and two-month-old daughter were staying with the Formans, tragedy enveloped the family.

Tom had been drinking steadily all day, getting more ill-tempered by the hour. That afternoon, he threatened his wife with violence and smashed some of the furniture. At the dinner table, Henry Forman finally took such exception to his son-in-law's attitude that he picked up his plate and went into the kitchen to eat alone. Schooley, an ugly look in his eye, staggered after Forman. Lounging in the doorway, he produced a revolver. Forman's fork was halfway to his mouth when Schooley fired. The bullet pierced Forman's hand, gouged the table and bounced into the wall. Forman jumped up and ran to the back door. As he reached it, another bullet ploughed into his back. With a gasp, he wrenched open the door and stumbled out. His wife and Ellen ran to help and summoned the doctor and police.

Dr. J.S. Helmcken's diagnosis was a gloomy one. He doubted that Forman would live through the night. Police inspector C.P. Bloomfield, accompanied by constables Clark, Beech and McPhee and the police magistrate, took the dying man's declaration and then turned his attention to the Forman house.

Schooley had locked all the doors. However, a knife blade under a kitchen window gained them entry. With the aid of their bull's-eye lamps, the squad searched the house. They found Schooley lying on his back on the floor, dead drunk, a two-gallon jug of port wine beside him, a loaded revolver in his hand. Another cocked and loaded revolver lay beside him on the floor, and in his pocket he had two loaded derringers. Schooley was soon disarmed and on his way to jail.

Forman died the next morning, and Schooley was charged with murder. It was now Penitent Tom who came up at the March assize to face a bench of judges that included Chief Justice Matthew Baillie Begbie, H.P.P. Crease and J. Hamilton Gray. Rocke Robertson did his best for the defence, stressing that it wasn't a crime of revenge, but a killing without malice aforethought. He spoke of Schooley's previous good character, his happy disposition and called for a verdict of manslaughter "prompted by the dictates of mercy."

"One man has died," he said to the jury. "Don't add to the crime and make it two deaths."

The jury took a mere 20 minutes to find Schooley guilty. When he was asked if he had anything to say before being sentenced, Happy Tom took the opportunity of explaining that he had purchased the derringers years before in San Francisco in anticipation of a trip to Nevada where "the highwaymen were reported active on the stage road."

Justice Gray, referring to this statement, noted:

No man requires to move about this community with firearms on his person; no man need carry a revolver or the life of another human being in his pocket. No stranger commentary than your remarks could be produced and if men act as you have done they will find that British law will drag down the highest that may dare to break it as it will lift up and protect the humblest who has trampled underfoot . . . Let the fate of this prisoner be a warning to men who carry firearms in any part of the province; they will be taught that when men take life they will be hanged as sure as there is a God in heaven!

Schooley found himself with just two months to live. On a morning in late May, he rose from his prison cot to take his last look at the blue sky and fleecy clouds. By 7:30 A.M., the roofs of buildings overlooking the jail yard were crowded with sightseers—people in a holiday mood, jocular and friendly. Inside the fence of the prison yard was a smaller crowd, invited in by a guard who swung the gate open. As the crowd waited, the masked executioner was in Schooley's cell, pinioning his arms with a leather belt. Provincial police superintendent John H. Sullivan nodded to a guard and the cell door opened. A few minutes later, Happy Tom was no more.

That November, two more Eureka shareholders met death. Frank Garesche and S.P. Moody, hoping to interest San Francisco capital in the Eureka Mine, took passage on the steamer *Pacific*, which collided with a sailing ship off Cape Flattery. Among those drowned were Garesche and Moody, and Superintendent Sullivan, who had supervised Schooley's hanging.

With four of its chief promoters dead, the Eureka didn't survive long, despite exceptional assay reports revealed in old records of the BC Department of Mines. With silver selling at $1.10 an ounce, the first shipment of ore assayed $460 a ton, "with thousands of tons of rock in sight." Once, two mules brought down a load that yielded 750 ounces of silver bullion. The first annual report of the Department of Mines in 1874 mentions a seam at the Eureka "four to seven feet in width, traced for 3,000 feet . . . the ore assaying from $20 to $1,050 a ton." The richer Van Bremner lead on the same property had run up to $2,400 a ton. Despite glowing reports, it was still a difficult task to bring out the ore. Finally, dissension among the owners caused a shutdown, and the stock slumped.

Maybe this unexpected financial setback mentally unbalanced the remaining original shareholder, George Deitz. Not long after, his wife made court application to have his affairs taken out of his hands. Without recovering, George died in California at 54.

In this aura of tragedy, the Eureka workings remained silent for the next 45 years, until the summer day in 1920 when A.S. Williamson rediscovered the mine. Acting as agent for Sperry and White in Seattle, he picked up the property in a tax sale. Plans were made to reopen the mine, but records show that nothing much happened. In 1935, the Department of Mines record ends laconically with "Struck off." British Columbia's first quartz mine had become just another hole in the ground, but not before tragically affecting the lives of its five promoters.

8

Death Be Not Denied

AN OLD PERSIAN FABLE TELLS of two rug dealers chatting in a bazaar. One of them suddenly spied Death on the edge of the crowd. "I must go," he said hurriedly to his companion. "I see Death approaching. I think he's looking for me."

"Where will you be safe?" asked his companion.

"In Samara. He'll never find me there."

With that he slipped into the crowd. A moment later, Death approached the man who remained. "Your friend disappeared before I could meet him," said Death. Then he added, "But it doesn't matter. I have an appointment with him tomorrow in Samara."

The records of the BC Provincial Police reveal that a German immigrant named Karl Fredericks had an experience similar to that of the rug dealer, except that his appointment with Death was not in Samara but in Nazi Germany.

The story opened on a sunny afternoon in late June 1930 in the central British Columbia village of Vanderhoof, gateway to a vast roadless area dotted with rugged peaks and slashed with huge lakes such as Stuart and Takla. In his office, Constable H.J. Jennings was having difficulty understanding what tall Anatole Matise of the Tachi band was telling him. It apparently involved a story of suspicion and mystery that was circulating around the fires at Tachi and other First Nations settlements. The Native people had decided to inform the white men of what had happened. From the Tachi River some 50 miles (80 kilometres) to the north, Anatole had slipped south by canoe until he arrived, smelling of sweat and woodsmoke, in the Vanderhoof police office. Here he related a story that might mean something— or nothing.

From what Constable Jennings could make out, a couple of weeks previously, three white men with a boatload of supplies had gone up the Tachi River, the link between Stuart Lake and Trembleur Lake. Two days later, one of the men returned and walked into the trading post of Cassiar Robert at Tachi village. He looked over the stock on the shelves and appeared to be in a spending mood. The stranger asked the price of a moosehide coat and when told it was $18, he promptly handed over the money. He then expressed interest in moccasins and gloves and was shown a few pairs of each. He bought the lot. Cassiar Robert noticed the man's 30-30 Winchester and offered to buy it for $20. He wouldn't sell, but a few minutes later, to Cassiar's surprise, the stranger swapped the rifle for another man's nearly worthless fox pelt. The Native man told him the pelt wasn't of much value, but the white man wanted it anyway.

Next, the stranger was intrigued with a pair of moose horns hanging on the wall. "There's a cache of food up the river you can have for those horns," he said. Cassiar was now not only surprised but also puzzled. A food cache could mean the difference between comfort or hardship, life or death. He was reluctant to clinch this deal. What about his partners? Wouldn't they need the food? The stranger made it plain, however, that the cache was his to dispose of. As proof, he wrote a pencilled authority on a slip of paper.

It was hard at times for Constable Jennings to know what Matise was getting at. The rambling story sounded like trading-post gossip. But as the man had come of his own will to tell it, there must be more. Jennings waited patiently. Matise went on to say that the Tachi men had asked the white man about his two companions. They were told they had gone up the lake with two Native boys as guides. Why was the stranger heading south? He was sick, he said.

"Where are you sick?" one man asked suspiciously. The white man pointed to his side. "Pain here," was his only comment.

The Tachi were too bush-wise to believe his explanation. They knew that only a healthy man could cover the Tachi Trail in two days, especially while carrying a pack. If his two companions had made a base camp on Trembleur Lake, why hadn't this man, if he was sick, used the boat to return south? And the story about two boys acting as guides was obviously a lie. An important celebration was planned for the next two days, and none of the Native boys would have gone anywhere if it meant missing the event of the year.

When the man's story was questioned, he showed signs of nervousness and broke off the conversation. The next day, he hired Peter Seymour to take him by boat to Fort St. James, where he grabbed his pack and moose horns and beat Seymour down a dollar in the fare. The last Seymour saw of him, he was hitching a lift to Vanderhoof in a light delivery truck.

After the stranger's departure, the Tachi mulled over the matter around the evening fire. The result was that Anatole Matise was delegated to inform the police at Vanderhoof of the incident and their suspicions. This he had now done, although when it came to describing the three men there was a baffling lack of detail. The best Matise could do was to catalogue the trapping trio as "one big man," "the middle-sized man" and "the little man." The man in the store was the middle-sized one.

From trapline records and information supplied by a Vanderhoof farmer, George Cameron, Constable Jennings pieced together the trio's identity. A month before, they had worked two weeks clearing land for Cameron and were paid $149 by cheque. The "tall man" was Max Westphal, a 6-foot (183-centimetre) German army veteran from the First World War. He was described as having a slow walk, an erect bearing, a clean-shaven face, sandy hair and a porcelain bridge on his upper front teeth. The "middle-sized" man was Karl Fredericks, 28, dark-haired and sallow-faced. He also was a German army veteran and had been in Canada only six months. Smallest of the three was Herman Peters, about Fredericks's age, aggressive, alert and probably leader of the trio. Peters was distinguished by a slight limp and widely spaced good teeth.

From these descriptions it was plain that the man who had returned was Fredericks. A check at the Vanderhoof railway station showed that he had bought a ticket for Edmonton. The station agent remembered him because of the moose horns he carried. "You can't check those as baggage," the agent had warned. "You'll have to send them on by express." In answer, the young man promptly tossed the horns into a nearby clump of brush.

Jennings reported this information to his district sergeant at Prince George, W.J. "Big Bill" Service. He instructed Jennings to go to Tachi and see what he could find out. When Jennings searched the southern margin of Trembleur Lake, he found the camp, the boat and a cache of food, but no signs of life. After two days of unsuccessful searching, it was plain to Jennings that any further investigation would have to be undertaken on a bigger scale with proper equipment. As a result, Inspector W.V.E. Spiller arrived from Prince George a week later with Sergeant Service and Constable J.H. McClinton. After a short conference in the little Vanderhoof police office, they headed for Tachi, where they interrogated the Tachi people, then pushed on to Trembleur Lake.

Spiller and Service criss-crossed the shoreline with a dragging device, hoping to snag the bodies of the missing men. They spent day after fly-bitten day sweating, heaving and rowing, but all that resulted was blistered hands. In the meantime, McClinton headed a party of Native men who combed the bush for miles around. They found no trace of the missing men. It was a disappointed police squad that finally arrived back in Vanderhoof. They had requested the Natives to watch for anything suspicious and from Vanderhoof sent out descriptions of the Fredericks and the missing men.

The Alberta Provincial Police quickly located Fredericks at Moon Lake, Alberta. He was not approached directly, but after circulating around the community for a day or two, a plainclothes policeman picked up the information that Fredericks mixed readily with settlers and talked occasionally of his trapping venture in British Columbia, although at times it was noted he gave conflicting answers to questions. He still had the mangy fox skin he got in exchange for the

Winchester rifle and persisted in saying that the HBC had offered him $10 for the pelt. He produced a watch that he said his girl had given him, although he occasionally forgot this story and said he had picked it off a dead comrade in the war. To one man, he mentioned a desire to change his name.

"A queer fellow," he was dubbed by the homesteaders, "never seems to tell the same story twice."

The BC Provincial Police, however, had nothing against Fredericks, and all they could do was to have Alberta's police keep him under observation. Thus matters remained until three months later. Early in November, Alex Prince, from Stuart Lake, arrived at the Vanderhoof police station. He had discovered what seemed to be a grave at Trembleur Lake.

With snow already knee-deep, it was not the best time to go looking for graves, although Prince said he had marked the site. Nevertheless, off went Constable Jennings and Prince. Three days later, they were farther up the lake than on the previous search. The snow was deeper still, but they finally found the markers. When Jennings removed some frozen moss he discovered fragments of underwear and a human limb. Prince watched as the policeman removed more rock and earth. A final tug on what appeared to be an old rag revealed that it enclosed a human skull.

Jennings had seen enough. Putting things back as he found them, he made a fast trip to Vanderhoof and returned with coroner W.R. Stone. There had been another snowfall, but with the aid of the markers they found the site. Two bodies were eventually uncovered.

At the autopsy in Vanderhoof, the remains were identified as those of the missing Germans, their teeth providing valuable clues. The coroner's jury decided that Westphal and Peters had been murdered "by a person or persons unknown . . . but evidence points strongly to the guilt of a man known as Karl Fredericks." The jury also commended the work of the provincial police, in particular Constable Jennings.

A wire to the Alberta Provincial Police quickly resulted in Fredericks's apprehension. Although formally warned, he stoutly maintained he did not know anyone called Westphal or Peters and had never been to Fort St. James, Trembleur Lake or Vanderhoof. He said he'd come to Moon Lake from the east and rode a freight train.

Constable McClinton went to Alberta to bring back the suspect, and as the foothills rolled past the car windows, Fredericks persisted in talking. But this time he told a different story. He admitted that he knew the dead Germans. All three had gone into the Trembleur Lake country to sell liquor to the Natives. Peters, he said, had a bad temper, and one day when they got to scuffling, Fredericks shot him in self-defence. When he returned to the lakeside camp, he discovered Westphal dead, apparently killed by Peters earlier in the day.

It was now five months since the double killing, and with Fredericks committed for trial, the Crown rested its case on the fact that Fredericks had concealed the bodies of his partners and failed to report their deaths. In addition, he had the watch belonging to one of the men, most of their money and had given away their cache of food. Physical evidence showed that the skulls of both men had been battered. Westphal's head had been severed from his body with a sharp instrument and wrapped in cloth and buried.

Peters's skull had a bullet hole in it and was smashed into 35 pieces. Dirt and twigs inside his shirt were considered evidence that the dead man had been dragged to his grave. Police and medical experts were of the opinion that the two men had been murdered in their sleep. From a layman's point of view, the affair was a double murder and a murderer's flight; from the legal profession's position, it wasn't that concrete. In fact, the subsequent courtroom tactics made legal history in British Columbia.

The tale of wilderness infamy unfolded in May 1931 when Karl Fredericks stood in the prisoner's box at the Prince George assizes. Because the prosecutor's case was part fact, part supposition, the jurors were unable to agree. A new trial was scheduled for the fall. This time the jury found Fredericks guilty and sentenced him to death. However, he appealed the decision and won a new trial at Kamloops. This jury overturned the sentence, and Fredericks walked from the courtroom a free man.

But his story didn't end there. As in the fable, Death was not to be denied. Two years later, Fredericks was picked up by Warden W.D. Quesnel near Bridge Lake in the Cariboo, a gun under his arm. Quesnel asked him if he had a licence. He hadn't. In addition, the warden discovered that Fredericks was an alien.

A Justice of the Peace sentenced him to a $50 fine or 60 days in jail. Fredericks decided to serve time—an unfortunate decision because when his picture and fingerprints were routinely passed on to Ottawa, they were matched to those of a man charged with murder some two years before. Since Fredericks was still a German national, Ottawa passed the information to the German police. They replied that he had had six convictions before he came to Canada.

Fredericks soon found himself in the hands of Canadian immigration officials, speeding across Canada to Halifax. He was aboard the next ship to Germany. It was a homecoming with grim undertones. In Fredericks's absence, a little man named Adolf Hitler had taken over the German Reich and was busily exterminating all opposition, especially communists. Unfortunately, before leaving his native land, Fredericks had done a little street fighting with the communists. As a consequence, two SS men, booted, belted and armed, were waiting at the gangway when Fredericks arrived in Hamburg. They promptly introduced him to the new order by whisking him off to a concentration camp.

It was the last ever seen of the man who dodged death in British Columbia only to keep an appointment in Hitler's version of Samara.

9

Whatever Happened to the Halden Family?

ON A MORNING IN EARLY April 1921, as a warm chinook wind steadily drove the snow from the Cariboo benchlands, BC Provincial Police sergeant George Hargreaves Greenwood of the Quesnel detachment received a letter he'd been anxiously awaiting. It was from Divisional Inspector W.L. Fernie at Kamloops. It said that a Mrs. Arthur Halden of Quesnel had previously been the widowed Mrs. Wright, and prior to that, in England, had been the spinster Adah Godfrey.

The excited Greenwood read the letter to his office companion, Constable E.E. Aves. "Don't you see it? Adah Godfrey: A.G. The initials on the ring."

For a moment Aves didn't understand, but then he

realized the significance of Greenwood's remarks. "And what are you going to do now, Sergeant?"

"You and I," said Greenwood, "are going to arrest Mr. David Clark."

Later in the day, Greenwood and Aves rapped on the door of the Grandview farm three miles (five kilometres) from Quesnel. A tall, dark and well-built man in his early thirties opened the door.

"You're under arrest, Clark, on a charge of theft," Greenwood said.

"Theft of what?"

"A couple of rings and a couple of brooches."

"Has Mrs. Halden come back?"

"No. She's not back."

"Then who laid the charge?"

"I did," said Greenwood, then added the time-worn formula, "You are not obliged to say anything in answer to the charge."

Thus did Sergeant George Greenwood make the Crown's opening move in an incredible story of murder, mystery and intrigue that went down in the records of the BC Provincial Police as "The Halden Case."

Dave Clark, so suddenly plucked from his doorstep by the police, had come to the Cariboo from the prairies the previous year, and in July had gone to work for the Haldens. The Haldens, a quiet couple in their mid-forties with a 14-year-old stepson, had come from southern British Columbia to take up land a few miles from Quesnel. The Haldens didn't go into Quesnel very often, but in late fall someone noticed that they hadn't been around at all. The hired man, Clark, explained that the three had suddenly gone to Spokane to attend the funeral of Halden's brother. A week or so after the family's departure, Clark met Greenwood in Quesnel.

"I've got a bit of a problem," explained the farm hand. "In the last few months I lent the Haldens quite a bit of money and now I'm getting worried."

"Worried? Why?" the sergeant asked.

"Well, I've got a hunch that they won't be coming back. So it looks as though I'm going to get stuck for over $1,000."

"Got anything in writing?"

"Yes," said Clark, drawing a folded paper from his pocket. "I've got their promissory note. It's properly signed and everything."

"I think you'd better see a lawyer," advised Greenwood. "He'll know what to do."

On the strength of this conversation with Greenwood, Clark contacted lawyer E.J. Avison. In the month that followed, he began a court action for the return of $1,250 loaned to the Haldens, and a claim for wages of $762 owing from April to December 1920.

Clark, under oath, claimed that, "On or shortly after October 29, 1920, the Haldens left for Spokane but notwithstanding most careful enquiries from the postmaster and all likely persons I cannot obtain any news of the whereabouts of the said defendants. I have ascertained they have left considerable obligations behind them and I believe they have left the country and do not propose to return."

He went on to declare, "I know of no way in which the summons in this action can be served and I respectfully apply for an order for service on them by deposit of summons in the Quesnel registry and by notice in the Cariboo Observer." The document was sworn to before government agent Edgar C. Lunn on December 8, 1920. In due course, County Court Judge Fred Calder granted permission to proceed with the action.

With these legalities behind him, bachelor Clark accepted an invitation to Christmas dinner at the neighbouring Andersons. Thoughtfully, Clark brought along Christmas stockings for the Anderson children and a present for Mrs. Anderson, carefully wrapped in tissue paper. It turned out to be a pretty horseshoe brooch set with pearls. Clark had also something for Mr. Anderson, a plain gold ring inscribed "A.G. for Father, 1892."

"Here, here," protested Anderson, "I can't take a thing like this. It must be some sort of family heirloom."

"Oh, no it isn't," laughed Clark. "As a matter of fact, I took it off a dead German officer in France."

That same evening, visiting other neighbours, Clark gave the wife of Captain W.E. Ekins, the local auctioneer, a handsome gold-plated 29th Battalion brooch.

A week later, the court-instructed advertisement appeared in a New Year's edition of the local *Cariboo Observer*. While there was no response from the Haldens, there were by now rumours circulating among the people who knew them. Eventually, some of this talk reached Greenwood. The account of Clark's generosity made Greenwood wonder. Then he connected it with the story of Clark's promissory note. But as Avison was handling it, everything seemed proper. In the days that followed, however, Greenwood couldn't help wondering about the Haldens and their sudden departure.

He called at the post office and found there had been quite a lot of mail for the Haldens during the previous summer but that it had dwindled when a number of letters had been returned to the senders marked "Left the district. No forwarding address." Greenwood's curiosity next took him to the telegraph office. A check of incoming telegrams around October 29 showed no message for the Haldens. In fact, no one in the district had received a telegram from Spokane. Greenwood's next stop was the telephone office, and there the answer was the same. There had been no long-distance call summoning the Haldens to a funeral in Washington.

It was all very queer and most mysterious. At his office, Greenwood cogitated and then came up with another idea. He would put in a report to his divisional officer and ask for a check on the Haldens' antecedents. All he could quote for identification was the fact that they owned Lot 6681, Group I, Cariboo District.

The report trickled down to the force's CIB headquarters in Vancouver, where a plainclothes man checked the land registry office. On the title deed was the rubber stamped names of Wallace and Van Roggen, the Vancouver law firm who had handled the land deal. In reply to the detective's questions, they said that they had conducted most of the Haldens' business but hadn't heard of them for some time. In fact, the last letter on file was dated June 2, 1920. Through the firm, however, Mrs. Halden's sister, Thurza Hughes, was located at Parksville on Vancouver Island. She too was mystified by her sister's sudden absence from Quesnel.

According to Mrs. Hughes, her sister Adah had been married to a Mr. Wright in England, and on his death in 1915 came to Vancouver with her stepson, Stanley. She worked for a while in Victoria, but contracted typhoid fever and spent time as a patient in the Royal Jubilee Hospital. Later, she convalesced at the Hughes' Parksville home and in 1919 met and married Arthur Halden. The couple lived at Wellington on Vancouver Island, then moved to Quesnel in the early spring of 1920.

Apparently Mrs. Halden still had money in England amounting to about $5,000. In May 1920, she thought of transferring these funds to a bank in Quesnel, but changed her mind when the rate of exchange took an adverse turn.

Meanwhile, she bought six $50 Victory Bonds for her stepson, and these were still in the Quesnel bank.

The police next probed Arthur Halden's background. They discovered that he had no brother in Washington, and official records confirmed that no one of that name had died in eastern Washington the previous fall. Furthermore, Spokane police said no one named Halden had registered at any Spokane hotel the previous October. After Greenwood analyzed this information, he checked locally and discovered that the family had stocked up with groceries just before their disappearance. If they intended to leave, why did they buy so many groceries?

Clark showed Thurza Hughes the ring that Clark had given away at Christmas. She promptly identified it as her sister's memorial ring on the death of their father in 1892. She also identified the pearl horseshoe brooch and produced a picture of her sister's wedding in Vancouver in 1919 that showed Adah wearing it.

With this information, Sergeant Greenwood had to act quickly before the Haldens' property became Clark's by due process of law. That was why he arrested Clark on April 17, 1921, for theft. Clark stuck to the story that he had taken the gold ring from a dead German during the war and vowed he had bought the brooch in England.

When Clark's case came before the Prince George spring assize in 1921, the jury could not agree. His lawyer applied for bail, but since Divisional Inspector Fernie would not consent to bail under $10,000, a sum that Clark could not raise, he stayed in jail. According to Fernie, the prospect of Mrs. Halden's money coming from England had spurred Clark to kill the family and lay claim to the estate. But if Clark had murdered the Haldens, how, when and where had he done it?

As Clark languished in jail that summer, squads of police criss-crossed the Halden farm and neighbouring countryside. They employed scores of skilled Native trackers in an attempt to pick up any fragments of information that might be the key to unlocking the Cariboo mystery. The farmhouse was searched from roof to basement. Walls were tapped, floors torn up and the earth floor of the basement excavated and sifted. Nearby ditches and sloughs were probed, and days were spent dragging nearby Dragon Lake. Wherever there was the appearance of a slash fire, the soil was sifted to a considerable depth. Wells were pumped and back eddies in the Quesnel River explored. After weeks of searching, however, the tired and frustrated provincial police had to admit the Halden family had vanished.

In November, Clark was tried for a second time, again at Prince George. On this occasion, however, he was found guilty and sentenced to two years in prison. While the smug-faced Clark spent his days in the turreted penitentiary on the banks of the Fraser at New Westminster, the police continued their search for the Haldens. A $1,000 reward was offered but failed to prompt any response. Another angle considered by the police was that if Clark had loaned the Haldens $1,250, he may have had a bank account. Asked about it in the penitentiary, Clark told the police with a smile that he didn't believe in banks. He always kept his money in a belt around his waist.

"You carried $1,250 around with you?" suggested the investigator.

"Sure," said Clark.

While searching the Halden farmhouse, the police couldn't help noting one significant fact. There wasn't a letter or a document in the place bearing the Halden signatures and not a single photograph of the couple. All had been destroyed, the twisted and melted picture frames found in the ashes of a bedroom heater.

Greenwood, however, made an interesting discovery. A blotter, held to a mirror, showed that someone had been practicing Halden's signature. Fortunately, the law firm of Wallace and Van Roggen had the authentic Halden signatures. These were checked with the signatures on Clark's promissory note, which a handwriting expert promptly branded as a forgery. So did Thurza Hughes, accustomed to seeing her sister's signature.

In the fall of 1923, the main gate of the penitentiary at New Westminster swung open to release Clark. His freedom was brief. Waiting was a provincial police sergeant with a warrant charging him with forgery. That December, before Mr. Justice Aulay Morrison and a New Westminster jury, David Arthur Clark stood, a half-quizzical smile on his face, and pleaded not guilty. Crown Counsel George Cassidy drew from witnesses one of the strangest stories aired in a British Columbia courtroom. It recounted those toilsome weeks around the Grandview farm where the police delved and probed for a trace of three people who the Crown were sure had been murdered. Perhaps the ghosts of the Haldens were hovering in the courtroom, especially when Clark's lawyer asked Mrs. Hughes why she referred to her sister as the "late" Mrs. Halden. "You have no proof that she is dead," he suggested.

"Oh, she's dead all right," was Mrs. Hughes quiet reply.

The motive for the forgery was reviewed, including Clark's brazen attempt to take over the estate of the missing couple through the Quesnel court action. "His clumsy efforts to delude the law were unavailing," was how Judge Morrison summarized it to the jury. On Friday, December 13, the jury retired. They returned in an hour with the verdict that David Arthur Clark was guilty.

"Have you anything to say before I pass sentence?" asked Judge Morrison. The entire court waited, expecting Clark to make some sort of admission.

With his customary smile, Clark bowed to the bench, "Your Lordship." Then, as an afterthought, he turned to the packed courtroom and added, "And ladies and gentlemen."

"You are not here to make a speech," said the judge, as he cut him off. "The law entitles me to give you a maximum sentence of fourteen years imprisonment. However, I'm not in agreement with long sentences, and I'm going to give you ten years."

It has been many decades since the Haldens vanished from their Quesnel homestead. No trace of them has ever been found.

10

A Policeman Dies

ON AN AFTERNOON IN LATE June 1887, a lone horseman galloped his sweat-streaked bay mount through the verdant bottomland of the lower Similkameen Valley in southern British Columbia. The impatient rider was a tall, lean cowpuncher named Frank Spencer, who was missing one finger. The horse he was riding was stolen and so was the saddle, bridle and the .44 Winchester in the scabbard alongside his leg.

Spencer was fleeing because he had shot and killed a fellow cowboy near Kamloops about a week before over a bottle of rye. But that wasn't his first lawless act. Orphaned in Tennessee, Spencer was already wild when he hit Texas at 16. From there, he brawled and gunfought until at 20 he was in Dodge City. Here, history reminds us, Marshall "Mysterious Dave" Mathers killed seven men in one night, and 25 men were killed and 50 wounded in one bullet-splattered year.

The youthful Spencer was jailed there a couple of times before moving on to Tombstone, Arizona, where he teamed up with the infamous Clanton gang to raid Mexican cattle ranches. But in 1881, the lawless element was decimated when the Earp brothers, along with "Doc" Holliday, took on the Clantons at the OK Corral; Jesse James was shot in Missouri; and Billy the Kid eliminated at White Oaks, New Mexico.

Frank Spencer got the message. In order to stay above ground, he made for southeastern Arizona, then drifted to Colorado and worked his way north to Montana. He was rustling horses there when members of the Stock Growers' Association decided to take the law into their own hands. Under the leadership of "Strangler" Stuart, the association hoisted a lot of characters up the nearest tree. All had the misfortune to have someone else's brand on their stock.

It was time for Spencer to move again. This time he crossed the Canadian line into the region that became Alberta. Finally, in 1886, he rode the first CPR train as far as Kamloops. Here, a year later, he shot and killed Pete Foster in the corral of Campbell's Ranch. He promptly left on one of Campbell's horses, pursued by BC Provincial Police constable Walter H. Smith and two Native trackers.

The lawman pursued him clear to the United States border, but without the aid of telephone or telegraph, there was little chance of interception.

Three years later, Spencer's luck was shattered by a provincial policeman with an uncanny memory. At the time, Spencer was working for a Pendleton, Oregon, horse breeder who was readying some horses to ship to New Westminster. Although Spencer, in occasional bunkhouse confidences, had hinted about being in trouble with the law in Canada, he now decided that was all in the past and agreed to travel north with the horses. One of his fellow horse wranglers remarked that he might be taking a bit of a chance. As he succinctly put it, "Up there in Canada, Frank, the law only gives you one shake of the dice." The words proved to be deadly prophetic.

On his second day in New Westminster, Spencer strolled into a bar on Columbia Street. He had just ordered a drink when a stranger touched him on the arm. The stranger identified himself as Constable Isaac Decker and informed Spencer that he was under arrest for the murder of Pete Foster at Kamloops some three years before.

If Spencer was flabbergasted, he had a right to be. He had never been in custody in British Columbia and perhaps only a dozen people around Kamloops would have recognized him. Yet this provincial policeman from Ashcroft who'd never seen Spencer before had picked him up by the description on a three-year-old circular. There had been no photo, just a written description of a murderer with a missing finger.

In the typically expeditious style of the day, within a month Spencer was tried at Kamloops spring assize. On the bench was Mr. Justice G.A. Walkem, who—probably to the prisoner's wonderment—was wearing a wig. The jury found him guilty, and 40 days later, Frank Spencer was hanged at the Kamloops jail. The tough cowboy from Dodge City and points south had one final but rather curious wish. He didn't want to die with his boots on, so wore carpet slippers to the scaffold and when he was buried in the jail yard.

Constable Decker, the policeman with the uncanny memory for circulars, served a few more years in the BC Provincial Police. Then he took up a ranch near Spences Bridge, 25 miles (40 kilometres) from Ashcroft.

In June 1909, two decades after the Spencer trial, Decker received a telegram from the district chief of provincial police at Ashcroft, Joe Burr, the great-uncle of Raymond Burr, who one day would portray on television the super-efficient attorney Perry Mason and the wheelchair sleuth Ironside. The telegram was short. Because of an emergency, could Decker fill in for a few days as a special constable? A CPR train had just been held up near Kamloops in the same manner and place where Bill Miner had held up a train three years before. Three men were said to be involved, and police thought there was a chance they might come down the Thompson River by boat. Decker promptly responded, and Burr posted him on the riverbank just outside Ashcroft.

A day later, around dusk, a skiff appeared with two men in it. When Decker spotted them, he pumped the lever action of his Winchester and yelled to the boatmen to come ashore. With some difficulty, the inexperienced oarsmen manoeuvered the boat to the shore and hauled it up the bank. As they walked toward him, Decker noticed one of them carrying a coat over his arm—a coat that Decker quickly realized screened a revolver. Decker fired from the hip, the .44 slug catching the coat-carrying man on the point of his chin. With split-second reaction, his partner returned the fire. Decker dropped, a bullet through his heart. The sole witness to this deadly gunplay was a Native woman leaning over the bridge nearby. She saw the survivor of the shootout stoop and take something from his dead companion's pocket. Then, with a sort of loping trot, he disappeared into a clump of willows.

A mounted posse, Native trackers and bloodhounds were soon combing the region. But though the search continued for weeks, the fugitive had simply vanished. There was one lead. A cheap suitcase found in the bandit's skiff yielded a snapshot of an unnamed group. Copies of the photo were sent to police on the US Pacific coast. It was finally linked to a house in Long Beach, California, where investigators discovered the parents of the train-robbing duo. They identified the dead man as Dave Haney; the fugitive was his older brother, William.

$4,000.00 REWARD $4,000.00

The Government of the Province of British Columbia hereby offers a reward of TWO THOUSAND FIVE HUNDRED DOLLARS for the arrest and conviction of WILLIAM HANEY, who, on the night of the 28th day of June, 1909, near Ashcroft in the said Province, shot and killed one Isaac Decker, a Special Constable.

In addition to the reward of Two Thousand Five Hundred Dollars, offered by the Government of British Columbia,

The Canadian Pacific Railway Co. offers a further reward of One Thousand Five Hundred Dollars

making a total reward of Four Thousand Dollars, payable on the terms above mentioned.

WILLIAM HANEY
PHOTOGRAPH TAKEN IN 1896

WILLIAM HANEY
LATEST PHOTOGRAPH OBTAINABLE

Description of WILLIAM HANEY American

AGE—About thirty-eight years.

HEIGHT—Five feet eight inches.

WEIGHT—About 180 pounds.

BUILD—Well built and muscular. Has slightly swinging, lazy walk, from side to side like a sailor; drags feet.

COMPLEXION—Medium.

HAIR—Mixed with grey. Slightly bald on crown, has "cowlick" and usually combs hair back. Forehead high at sides.

EYES—Blue, almost grey.

FACE—Broad, flat features. Nose normal between eyes, but grows quite large at end—end of nose red and fleshy. Large nostrils. Large ears. **TWO MOLES ON RIGHT CHEEK.**

HANDS—Thick, fat hands; hair on hands quite thick and coarse.

MARKS—Large mole on top of right shoulder. Large vaccination mark on right upper arm. One small scar back of head.

Wire any information to the undersigned.

By Order,

F. S. HUSSEY,
Superintendent, Provincial Police.

Provincial Police Department,
Victoria, B. C.
3rd August, 1909.

WINTER EDITION

Despite the $4,000 reward offered for William Haney's capture, he was never seen again. BC ARCHIVES I-68387

Haney was never caught. Even though the search lasted 10 years, he never appeared in any North American prison or police station—or anywhere else. The British Columbia government and the CPR posted rewards totalling $4,000 for his capture. In addition, the CPR set aside $2,500 to help educate Isaac Decker's son, Archie, who was 12 when his father died in the line of duty.

The CPR intended to offer Archie a job when he graduated from school. However, in 1914, the First World War intervened. A year later, young Archie joined the army and was posted to France with the 1st Pioneer Battalion in March 1916. Brief, however, was his share of life. He was killed in action three months later. Father and son deserve a memorial for service to their country.

11

The Unfortunate Jerry Hill and Free Enterprise

"THE KOOTENAYS," PIONEER NEWSPAPER editor Bob Lowery once remarked, "are short of frills, boiled shirts, parsons, lawyers and prohibition orators, but plentifully supplied with mule skinners, packers, trail blazers and remittance men." This summary by a newspaperman who became a legend is a good introduction to the thousands of free-swinging, hard-drinking characters who built the CPR in the early 1880s and in whose polyglot wake shantytowns like Summit City in Rogers Pass and Farwell on the Columbia River sprang into prominence. Today, Farwell—now Revelstoke—lives only in historic photographs and newspaper clippings, but during its brief existence it became somewhat infamous. It was the site of a confrontation between the BC Provincial Police, the

North West Mounted Police (NWMP) and a force known as "Dominion Constables."

Some say the Farwell affair stemmed from a clash between federal and provincial liquor laws. Maybe so. At that time in the Northwest Territories (the prairies), there was theoretical prohibition, whereas British Columbia law allowed people to drink anything, anywhere, anytime, so long as they paid for it.

Licensees, at least in the Kootenays, had to provide accommodation for a minimum of six guests. Along the line of construction camps, this requirement was easily met by putting six cots at the end of the barroom and screening them with a sheet. While not providing much privacy, the arrangement did comply with the law. The proprietor's wife often sat up half the night dealing stud poker (appropriating 10 percent from every pot), while her husband tended the bar. This happy situation could go on night and day, seven days a week.

The provincial police, very few and very scattered, were strung from the Rockies to the coast and only interceded in a fight when some spoilsport drew a gun or a knife, or was caught in an act of thievery, considered an exceedingly low crime.

In 1885, interior papers reported with crisp economy of words such doings as: "Frank Hutchins came to town . . . was indulging too freely on Sunday; Monday morning his body was found near the north side of Main Street. He is believed to have fallen and broken his neck. Buried at government expense."

At Fort Steele: "A few days ago Joe, a half-breed packer for R.L. Galbraith, stabbed his brother-in-law on the Kootenay River. While Mr. Rykert was viewing the body the murderer went out and hanged himself."

Near Eagle Pass, "William Leonard quit work on the 24th, and was found two weeks later three-quarters of a mile from the river, a bullet in the back of his head. Been dragged off the road and dumped in the bush. He was a whisky peddler."

At Black Canyon on the CPR line, Bill Ableshire killed a man called Carey in a gladiatorial shovel-versus-knife fight, and when a Shuswap ferryman picked a fight with a passenger, shotgun versus revolver, "Provincial Constable Charles Todd reached out his hand for the revolver saying, 'I'll take the pistol, you take a sleep,' and the danger was over."

This was the year a lone American traveller named Baird was found dead at Kicking Horse Pass near Golden, and his murderer, "Bulldog" Kelly, was pursued clear to Minneapolis. On the North Thompson River, John Everson killed Louis Wallshed and vanished to Victoria. There, two months later, he was picked up as he window-shopped in Trounce Alley.

Another newspaper account related how provincial constable Jack Kirkup arrived in Kamloops with William Brown, who was "accused of murdering Mary Purcell in the Montana Saloon," a mere tent in the mountains, and brought along with him for good measure "The Big Kid," who got three years for theft, and "Shoo Fly," locked up for 18 months for drawing a gun on a constable.

These were a few of the year's social highlights when on an afternoon in mid-July in 1885, Irish-born Jerry Hill innocently rode into Farwell with eight cases of whisky on two pack horses and an unshaken belief in the free enterprise system. The uproar he caused was truly astonishing, especially since a provincial liquor licence in his pocket proved that he was no bootlegger.

Jerry Hill was going into business where the railroaders were thickest, although only construction trains were running. He was also triggering a bureaucratic nightmare. As an aid to sobriety, the Dominion government had established small NWMP detachments between Donald and Farwell. Unfortunately, Louis Riel's rebellion had caused the Mounties' commanding officer, the efficient Sam Steele, to be hurriedly called east that April. In his place had come George Hope Johnston, gazetted at Ottawa in May as a "Commissioner of Police for British Columbia" and a Justice of the Peace. One immediate problem was that Ottawa had no business—or right—to appoint a British Columbia commissioner of police. Nevertheless, Johnston immediately strengthened Farwell's four-man NWMP detachment with additional "Dominion Constables."

Although Ottawa had proclaimed a ban on liquor for

10 miles (16 kilometres) on each side of railway construction, the Mounties quickly found the edict as hard to enforce as it was on the prairies. However, Johnston enthusiastically settled to the task of eradicating the demon rum—or anything else alcoholic. As a consequence, one afternoon Jerry Hill was summarily relieved of his cargo.

A little puzzled, and displaying his British Columbia liquor licence, Hill went to see the magistrate, Malcolm Sproat. Assisting Sproat were provincial constables Jack Kirkup, John "Paddy" Miles and Arthur Hubbard. Ontario-born Kirkup, diplomatic and muscular, was to become something of a legend in British Columbia law enforcement. One of his accomplishments was keeping the peace in the mining community of Rossland, unaided. Since he weighed 300 pounds (136 kilograms), it wasn't surprising. British Columbia historian Elsie G. Turnbull wrote, "Constable Kirkup treated the unruly element with a heavy hand. His method of control consisted of 'pounding, instead of impounding, offenders.'"

Kirkup's answer to drunkenness was to lock up the drunk, then go after the saloon keeper. "Many a bartender learned to keep his difficult customers out of sight until they were normal again," Turnbull noted. "Kirkup sometimes encouraged 'tanked' miners to fight, believing a little exercise would help work the whisky out of their pores. If men were long on talk and short on performance it wasn't unknown for Kirkup to bump heads together until he got them mad and then set them down to finish it."

Constable Jack Kirkup was renowned for singlehandedly enforcing the law in the rowdy mining community of Rossland. BC ARCHIVES A-02263

Then there is the story of a boxing match in Rossland staged by two shysters from Spokane. Unfortunately for them, Kirkup was chosen to referee. Knowing that they had been faking their bouts, he brought them together in the ring. "Boys," he said quietly, "I don't want to see any flim flam here. I want to see a spirited exhibition. And to ensure that it is, the loser's going to get three months in jail."

With strong-willed provincial policemen such as Kirkup backing Magistrate Sproat, who undoubtedly resented the federal intrusion into provincial domain, a judicial conflagration quickly erupted over Jerry Hill and his attempt to embrace free enterprise. The precise facts are hard to unravel, but a man called Ruddick was involved, who was probably one of Johnston's Dominion constables. BC Provincial Police constables Miles and Hubbard had a warrant for Ruddick, on account of Jerry Hill's rightful complaint that Ruddick had lifted his booze.

The provincial constables found Ruddick, but in a rapid change of events, their prisoner was wrested from them, and they were imprisoned in the NWMP barracks. Miles, in some ingenious fashion, escaped to report the story to Sproat. Hubbard, meanwhile, was summarily sentenced to 14 days by Johnston—not a friendly way to treat a police-man who was simply carrying out his orders.

The fact that an NWMP sergeant was arrested by Kirkup late that night probably had little bearing on the matter. The sergeant had imbibed a little too freely in one of the local gin mills and fell through the window of a Chinese laundry while making his way home. Though embarrassing, it was something that could have happened to anyone. Equally embarrassing to the federals was that the next morning an NWMP corporal came to explain to the provincial police that the sergeant was needed as a witness in a case. "Have him back here in an hour," was Kirkup's edict, and apparently the gentlemanly agreement was adhered to.

The jailing of Hubbard, however, was more serious, especially as the constabulary byplay had become common knowledge, and the town was in a bit of an uproar. Johnston and his Dominion police force were virtually besieged. Kirkup suggested swearing in about 20 special constables and storming the federal bastille, but Sproat had a more legal approach. He issued warrants for the arrest of Johnston and his two chief assistants, Rhodes and Fane. Kirkup made the arrests, unaided. He was all policeman.

One comical aspect in the now ridiculous affair was when Sproat sent a man called Garden, with a white flag of truce, to get some of Johnston's personal belongings. The lockup door was opened a crack and a gun stuck in Garden's face. "Garden, being an old soldier," runs the official report, "merely laughed."

Sproat reported the situation to the Attorney General in Victoria, intimating that everything was under control and no assistance was needed, although he did say "he [Johnston] threatened to arrest myself and every officer connected with the province . . . he and his men marched into the chief streets of town like cowboys on a raid." Of the "siege" he noted, "These policemen seem frightened out of their wits by their situation before the law and the prompt incarceration of their ringleader."

When news of the constabulary crisis reached Ottawa, Colonel James F. Macleod, a former commissioner of the NWMP, promptly appeared. Macleod, a level-headed man, seems to have soon realized that the representatives of the Dominion government were far from capable. The problem the two men had to resolve, Sproat noted in formal but somewhat confusing language, was that there "was no question of con-stitutionality of acts and no question as to the license involved in the offence which was simply a flagrant obstruction of the administration of provincial justice in its temperate exercise."

In plain words, the now-baffled Jerry Hill and his valid liquor licence were of secondary importance—the obstruc-tion of the BC Provincial Police was the point at issue. Macleod apparently felt the same way. Sproat told Victoria that "neither the officer commanding the North-West Mounted Police here nor anybody else competent to judge attempts to defend the dominion police." Johnston, mean-while, sitting in his provincial cell, must have wondered how he got into such a muddle so quickly.

Sproat asked Colonel Macleod to sit on the case with him; as he put it, sitting alone he could only commit the accused to the next Kamloops assize. Two magistrates, however, could deal with the accused immediately. As a consequence, on the morning of August 30, 1885, Sproat and Macleod took their places on the bench to view a motley group that included four uniformed Mounties and a very downcast Johnston. He pleaded not guilty but then changed his mind and entered a guilty plea.

He was charged with obstructing provincial constables John Miles and Arthur Hubbard and "aiding and abetting the release of James Ruddick." Constable Kirkup addressed the court with the suggestion that the charges be reduced to common assault. "Do you speak on behalf of the two Constables aggrieved?" asked Magistrate Sproat.

"I do," said Kirkup. "They don't wish for a vindictive penalty, but only ask that their position be made clear."

With this request granted, Magistrate Sproat then spoke of the seriousness of the offence and the fact that it was punishable by six months of hard labour and, if need be, a $100 fine, which was over four months' pay for a Mountie. "The position I make clear in a few words," he concluded. "A notion prevails that in these cases there is a question between the Dominion and the Province. This is not so. It is the law of Canada that is concerned, the law that I chiefly administer in this court and as a token of the unity and diversity of our Canadian institutions, I am glad that, in these cases today, to have associated with me a distinguished judge from a sister territory on the other side of the mountains." On this gracious and amiable note,

"Commissioner of Police" Johnston, guilty of three charges of assault, was fined $10 on each count, plus $9.75 costs.

Colonel Macleod then left the bench, and Magistrate Sproat addressed himself to the four Mounties, who had all pleaded guilty: "I am remitting you all to your officers for trial." The last word came from Kirkup, who reminded the court that Johnston's Dominion constables had all fled town, including the five who put Constable Paddy Miles in a cell. "Prepare warrants for their arrest," ordered Sproat.

"Thus," the Kamloops paper later noted, "ended a somewhat startling action on the part of the magistrate but the authority of his court had been memorably and completely vindicated."

Johnston slipped quietly away, and in due course the Mounties welcomed back the much more capable Sam Steele. While no grudges apparently surfaced over the affair, neither did Jerry Hill's liquor. In some suspicious manner, the constabulary lost it in the shuffle. The sequel, however, was almost as funny as the siege of Farwell.

A Victoria citizen who put up the money for the liquor took legal action against Jerry Hill, who by now must have had his faith in free enterprise somewhat shattered. That fall, provincial constable George Wright at Kamloops found a writ of capias in his mail. More familiar with cattle brands than capias, Wright consulted government agent Tunstall, who said, "It's an authority to hold Jerry until the debt's satisfied. You'll have to lock him up."

To the free and easy Constable Wright, this action seemed hardly in keeping with the code of the West. He compromised. Jerry was to turn up at the provincial jail every night to be locked up, but he could spend his days as he pleased. A time limit of three months was agreed upon. Thus, Jerry propped up the bar of Ned Cannell's Saloon by day and each night banged on the jail door for entry. One spring night, as the snow melted on the benchlands, a note was found on Jerry's cell bunk. It said simply that now that it was spring it was time for him to go, and thanks very much for the kind treatment.

Wright scratched his head and thought of the Victoria creditor. Surely there must be some sort of legal termination to this quaint deal. He consulted Tunstall again. "Send the sheriff at Victoria a bill for three months' board and lodging," said Tunstall with a grin, 'and I'll bet you never hear another word." They never did.

A few months later, the chime whistle of the first transcontinental train was heard through the mountain passes of the Rockies, by which time the Supreme Court of Canada had ruled that British Columbia controlled its own liquor laws. In a way, this ruling makes Jerry Hill the patron saint of the BC Liquor Control Board. But Jerry, like everyone else involved, was probably far more interested in forgetting his venture into private enterprise than being a saint.

12

The Cariboo's Stagecoach Bandits

FOR SOME 50 YEARS FROM the early 1860s to the First World War, the Cariboo Wagon Road from Yale to Barkerville, 400 miles (645 kilometres) to the north, was the main street of miners, cattlemen, settlers and all others who ventured into the Cariboo. Today a paved highway, the historic road has probably seen more types of transportation than any other in North America.

At first men walked over the route, their possessions on their back. One of them, Billy Ballou, became the first mailman, carrying letters the long distance to Barkerville for $1 each. Other means of transportation were camels, steam-traction engines, pack horses, dog sleds and huge wagons drawn by horses, mules and oxen. Here, too, were the yellow and red stagecoaches of the BC Express Company, the famous "BX" that operated on a regular schedule, whatever the weather. In the early 1860s, stagecoach service began from Yale and continued until construction of the CPR in the early 1880s destroyed the Cariboo Wagon Road through the Fraser Canyon. Then service began at a new community called Ashcroft and continued for another 30 years until completion of the Pacific Great Eastern Railway ended the stagecoach era.

During the decades of service, the BX built an outstanding reputation for reliability and service. In 1866, the New Westminster paper, the *British Columbian*, commented:

> It only remains to give a few figures, in order to afford the reader an idea of the present magnitude of the institution, and the success with which it has met under the able management of Mr. Barnard and Messrs. Dietz & Nelson. The number of miles traveled during the present year is 110,600. Number of men employed, exclusive of agents whose time is not entirely devoted to the Express, 38. Number of horses employed in the Express service, 160. Number of Expresses despatched from the head office in New Westminster during the present year, 450. Total amount of treasure and valuables, exclusive of merchandise, passing through the Express during the present year, $4,619,000.

In all, the stagecoaches carried tens of millions of dollars' worth of gold from the Cariboo creeks to Yale and

Ashcroft. At first, a mounted provincial policeman rode with the stage as escort during the months when the heaviest gold shipments were made, but after several years the service was discontinued because it was considered an unnecessary expense. After that the drivers were on their own. There were remarkably few robbery attempts, and only one could be considered a success, although the robber must have wondered just how successful it was as he later peered through prison bars.

One would-be robber was foiled because the driver, Charles Westoby, was deaf. As the story goes, on one trip his six-horse team bolted. Charles, thinking that they were running away for no good reason, grabbed his whip. As he plied the whip, he howled in rage, "I'll teach these sonsabitches to run away!"

When Charles got to the bottom of a mile-long grade, the blown and sweating cayuses settled to a canter. "That'll teach 'em," yelled Charles to his companion, unaware that the man beside him had been trying to explain why the horses had stampeded. Charles hadn't seen a masked man spur his horse out of a gully and try to intercept the stage. The road agent's warning shot caused the runaway, but Charles hadn't heard it. His disability on this occasion, however, earned him a handsome cheque.

On June 25, 1894, a robber named "Red Bluff" Charlie had better luck—but not much—when he held up the stagecoach at 150 Mile House and escaped with $45.

He was captured the next day. On July 4, he faced Judge Clement F. Cornwall and was promptly sentenced to 10 years in prison.

Although the bandit didn't realize it, he was lucky to be alive. The driver of the stagecoach he held up was Ed Owens, a quiet man who always carried a six-gun in the waistband of his trousers. He was a deadly shot, demonstrating his ability to passengers by knocking over grouse as the stage rolled along. During the holdup, the bandit ordered Owens to get the safe containing the gold, which he did, at the same time planning to draw his revolver and kill the robber. One passenger, however, was afraid of being hurt if shooting started and put a restraining hand on him. Owens hesitated, then decided to let the bandit live.

A duo which proved to be a man and a woman pulled the last holdup of His Majesty's Mail coach on November 1, 1909, some 8 miles (13 kilometres) south of 150 Mile House. They also had the tough luck to run into Charles Westoby. The result was described by Willis J. West, then general manager of the BX:

> The regular stage with a full load of passengers left the 150 Mile House early that morning. It was still dark when the stage approached a point on the road where there was a big tree on one side and a big boulder directly opposite. The woman, dressed like a man, waited behind the tree and the man behind the boulder. When the stage reached them, they both stepped out and covered the driver with their rifles.

The man then demanded all the registered mail sacks from 150 Mile House and points north.

Charles Westoby, the driver, who was quite deaf, pretended he could not understand their instructions. In the confusion he managed to keep back some of the registered sacks and substitute "empties" that were being returned to the railway. No attempt was made to rob or molest the passengers. Westoby was ordered to drive on and the stage made good time to the 134 Mile House, the nearest telegraph office. Here word was sent to all telegraph stations up and down the road notifying the police.

A posse was formed of B.X. employees and ranchers and proceeded to the scene of the hold-up. The police had already arrived to discover that the bandits had taken the mail-sacks a short distance into the brush, coolly cut them open, taken any currency from the letters, but left bank cheques and money-orders. The posse and the police tracked the bandits' barefooted horses for some miles until they encountered the tracks of a band of wild horses, obliging them to turn back and abandon the pursuit.

The country around 150 Mile House was at that time very sparsely settled. By careful checking and a process of elimination the authorities finally decided that the culprits were a woman and a man whom she called her brother-in-law who had been in the district only a few weeks. The pair were arrested and their cabin searched but the only evidence found was two freshly shod saddle-horses. After consultations with police headquarters in Victoria, the prisoners were brought down to Ashcroft, put on the train and told to get out and stay out of Canada. They were undoubtedly guilty and were obviously relieved to get off so lightly. It was estimated that they got only about $2,000. They missed one package of $5,000 in currency from the bank in Quesnel owing to driver Westoby's initiative in withholding some of the registered sacks.

The bandit who put the most original thought into his robbery was Martin Van Buren Rowland, a small barrel-chested man with a black beard. He was lucky enough to select a stage that didn't have Westoby as driver, although he perhaps would have been better off if he had. Rowland's problem turned out to be Frederick S. Hussey, a powerfully built policeman who rose from the ranks to head the force. In 1891, he was in charge of the vast Kamloops region with the rank of chief constable.

It was hot in the British Columbia interior that summer, and by mid-August cattlemen were declaring it was the driest spell in 50 years. Stage driver Steve Tingley, southbound to Ashcroft, was also feeling the heat. He reined in his six horses at Bridge Creek near 100 Mile House to give them a breather before tackling the hill ahead. As he reached for a chew of Mail Pouch, he was surprised by a rather peremptory order: "Stick up your hands!"

As Steve wrapped his reins around the brake handle, then reached skyward, he glimpsed by a roadside stump the gleaming barrel of a Winchester and behind it the crouching figure of a man.

Slowly the bandit emerged from his ambush, a five-gallon hat shading his eyes, a red bandana over the lower part of his face. He was on the small side and rather thickset.

"All right," he drawled from behind the mask, "throw down the box."

"Ain't got no box," said Steve perfunctorily, matching the utterance with an equally casual squirt of tobacco juice, his hands still shoulder-high. The eyes between the hat brim and the red bandana assumed a rather steely look.

"Throw down that box or I'll blow your head off!" came the rougher command. There was just enough authority in the tone to help Tingley make up his mind. The small iron-bound box containing the gold dust was heaved to the ground.

When news of the robbery reached Ashcroft, the alarm went out swiftly. The two constables at 150 Mile House, Bill Parker and Fred Rose, immediately started scouting the plateau trails for sign of the lone bandit. At the same time, the constables at Quesnel and Barkerville were alerted. Constable Joe Burr at Ashcroft set out with a posse and found the strong box, minus its $5,000 to $6,000 in gold. But as the days lengthened into weeks with no further lead, it seemed as though the undersized bandit had vanished.

Two months later, word came of a fabulously rich new gold strike on Scotty Creek, which runs into the Bonaparte River between Ashcroft and Clinton. It appeared that a man called Rowland had hit the golden jackpot. Men who still had memories of the Cariboo gold rush made hasty plans to stampede to the new find. Rowland, meanwhile, casually hung around Ashcroft, standing rounds of drinks for his well-wishers. Apparently he was on his way to Vancouver to interest some mining men in what promised to be one of the richest strikes in Cariboo history.

While all this was going on, Chief Constable Hussey walked into the police office at Ashcroft late one afternoon to see if Burr had picked up anything further on the Bridge Creek robbery. In time, the conversation turned to Rowland and his gold strike. "You think he's really struck something?" said Hussey.

"Looks like it," said Burr, "and it must be pretty rich, the way he's spending around town."

Hussey went over to the window to stare into the street. Something nagged at his mind. For one thing, he remembered hearing that the Chinese had pulled out of Scotty Creek a year ago. After every big cleanup, the last to leave were the Chinese, who panned the stream for bare day wages. When the Chinese left, it was a sure sign that nothing of value remained. And there was something else wrong. A man who makes a strike doesn't usually come out and tell the world about it. Not right away, that is. Still another point was vaguely disturbing. The man who held up the stage at Bridge Creek was small and thickset, and so was Rowland.

"When did you say Rowland was leaving town?" remarked Hussey as he turned from the window.

A saloon in Ashcroft, perhaps the one patronized by the suddenly wealthy Martin Rowland. BC ARCHIVES C-08207

"From what he said he was leaving tonight," said Burr, "on the midnight train."

"Do you know where he left his gold for safekeeping?"

"I did hear he left it at Foster's store," said Joe.

Hussey looked at his watch. It was nine o'clock. With an impatient gesture, the police chief picked up his hat and shot a quick command at Burr. "Come on, Joe. Let's find the magistrate and get a warrant for Rowland for that stage robbery."

"But, chief," Joe protested, "we haven't got any evidence."

Hussey cut him short. A half hour later, with a warrant

in his pocket and a rather confused Joe Burr at his side, the police chief was heading for Rowland's hotel room. The little bearded miner was asleep on his bed when they entered.

"Me rob a stage?" he said, when he was fully awake. "You must be out of your mind."

"Maybe," said Hussey as he ran his hand under the blankets, then the mattress, then the pillow. He touched something hard, something that turned out to be a loaded .45 revolver.

The trio headed for the police station, stopping on their way at Foster's store. "Mr. Rowland would like the leather bag he left here for safekeeping," said Hussey, then took possession of it. At the police station, Rowland's manner changed. He wanted to make a written statement. Hussey obligingly supplied him with pen and paper. For the best part of an hour, Rowland wrote the story of his mining career that ended with the Scotty Creek bonanza. When he finished, he handed the pages to Hussey, who witnessed his signature. Then Joe Burr took him off to a cell.

By the light of an office oil lamp, Hussey scanned Rowland's story, Burr waiting for him to finish. When the police chief got to the last page, he said with a smile of satisfaction, "This fellow doesn't know the first thing about mining. He proved it when he wrote this. Now bring that lamp over here, and let's have that bag of Rowland's gold."

As the golden grains sprinkled over the table, Hussey produced a magnifying glass from his pocket and studied

Foster's store at Ashcroft in 1890, where Martin Rowland left his stolen gold for safekeeping. CITY OF VANCOUVER ARCHIVES

them carefully. He knew that each creek puts its own imprint on the gold it yields—a form of natural fingerprinting—and veteran miners can tell whether a poke of gold came from one creek or several.

"Just as I thought," he remarked, as he straightened from his task. "This is gold from different creeks. This stuff came out of that strongbox on the stage!"

That fall, the man who had struck it rich on Scotty Creek was tried at the Clinton assize. Steve Tingley recognized Rowland's voice and so did some of the passengers. But the clincher was the gold, and a jury of veteran Cariboo prospectors noted the evidence that the gold came from more than one source. They brought in a verdict of guilty, and Martin Van Buren Rowland got five years.

Epilogue

ON MAY 6, 1865, NEAR Bella Coola, BC Provincial Police constable John D.B. Ogilvie was shot aboard the schooner *Langley* by Antoine Lucanage. Despite Ogilvie's mortal wounds, he grappled with the cutthroat and fired two shots at him before collapsing. The constable was taken below deck, where he died within minutes. Lucanage escaped in a skiff.

Ogilvie was the first lawman murdered in British Columbia. The murder stirred the colony, and the government offered a $1,000 reward for Lucanage's capture. Despite the reward and a protracted search, he was never found alive, although he was variously reported as far south as San Francisco. Several months later, a corpse was found

on northern Vancouver Island and identified as Lucanage.
How he died remains a mystery, and the reward was never
claimed.

Many members of the BC Provincial Police died in the
performance of their duty, expecting nothing more than
that they be remembered. Here are their names:

Constable John D.B. Ogilvie, Bella Coola, May 1865
Constable John Lawson, Wildhorse Creek, April 1867
Constable John T. Ussher, Kamloops, December 1879
Constable Isaac Decker, Ashcroft, June 1909
Constable Geoffrey H. Aston, Okanagan Lake, March 1912
Constable Alexander Kindness, Clinton, May 1912
Constable Henry Westaway, Union Bay, March 1913
Constable George Stanfield, Grand Forks, June 1920
Constable Arthur W. Mable, Kamloops, September 1926
Constable Percival Carr, Merritt, May 1934
Inspector William J. Service, Prince Rupert, July 1938
Sergeant Robert Gibson, Prince Rupert, July 1938
Constable Clifford A. Prescott, Princess Royal Island, June 1939
Constable Frank Clark, Victoria, November 1941

Selected Bibliography

Books

Baillie-Grohman, W.A. *Fifteen Years' Sport and Life in the Hunting Grounds of Western America and British Columbia*. London: Horace Cox, 1900.

Bancroft, Hubert H. *History of British Columbia 1792–1887*. San Francisco: The History Company, 1887.

Downs, Art. *Wagon Road North: Historic Photographs from 1863 of the Cariboo Gold Rush*. Surrey: Heritage House, 1993.

West, Willis J. *Stagecoach and Sternwheel Days in the Cariboo and Central B.C.* Surrey: Heritage House, 1985.

Newspapers

British Columbian

Cariboo Observer

Index

Acknowledgements
to the 1993 Edition

In assembling material for this book, though many of the latter-day stories come from personal first-hand knowledge, those stemming from an earlier period required a good deal of research in the British Columbia Archives. I would indeed be remiss, therefore, if I failed to acknowledge my deep sense of gratitude to the late provincial archivist Willard Ireland and the very capable archives staff.

I also wish to thank the original publisher of these articles, *The Islander*, Sunday magazine of the Victoria *Daily Colonist*, for permission to reprint them, and also Gray's Publishing Ltd. of Sidney, BC, who presented many of them in an out-of-print, hard-cover book, *Tales of the British Columbia Provincial Police*.

About the Author

Born on November 11, 1899, in North Berwick, Scotland, Cecil (Nobby) Clark was 17 when he enlisted as a constable in the BC Provincial Police. He served for 35 years—more than one-third of the force's 92-year history—rising to the rank of deputy commissioner. After Clark's retirement in 1950 his service didn't end, it simply changed direction. Since the force had only about 100 members when he joined, he knew many of the pioneer policemen and worked on the later cases, interrogating rum-runners, thieves and murderers. He became the force's unofficial historian, creating a popular series of out-of-print books, *BC Provincial Police Stories*, that cover a fascinating cross-section of the force's cases. He died in 1993.